"This book is a superb refere: their families, for those who ᵥᵥᵤᵤᵤᵤ ᵥᵥᵤᵤᵤᵤ ᵤᵤᵥᵨᵨᵨᵨ and assist our law enforcement officers, and for our whole society in these times when the role of the law enforcement officer has become a matter of great public concern. I'm honored to know that my work could be of some assistance, in this worthy endeavor."

- Lt. Colonel Dave Grossman, Author, On Killing

"Traumatic Stress within the policing environment is a real injury. Although there are no slings, crutches or bandages the consequences can be far reaching to the point where suicide may be the only option of consideration for the involved member. "The Price They Pay" is a unique blend of impactful short stories mixed with educational portions on what Post Traumatic Stress actually is and how it invades the very being of individual police officers during their careers. Left untreated it can lead to disastrous consequences for the member, their family and co-workers. We must remember that our police personnel are 'Heroes in Life…Not Death.'"

- Sgt. Bill Rusk, Executive Director, Badge of Life Canada

"Karen and Jeff touch on many subjects NOT discussed by most law enforcement agencies. Most of us in the law enforcement community, know what little support we get from the media. Law Enforcement is now in the cross hairs of many politicians. In addition, many LEOs do not receive the proper support from their own department or their community. We (LE) fight every day to protect the innocent and not so innocent. This book describes how many in the Law Enforcement community do not receive the protection they deserve. Karen's dedication to the Law Enforcement community is refreshing! The material in this book would benefit current LEOs as well as new hires. I would like to thank Karen and Jeff for their effort in addressing mental health and law enforcement!"

- *John McClanahan*
Deputy Sheriff, 15 years

"Karen Solomon and Jeffrey McGill have effectively captured and shared the powerful stories of the emotional, psychological, physiological, relational, and spiritual consequences of a career in law enforcement in their book The Price They Pay. Our nation's police officers are now confronted with an increase in some of the most challenging and potentially deadly situations and encounters in our history. It is imperative that all officers recognize and embrace the impact of their chosen profession so that they may strive to make better and more resilient choices to not only survive but thrive in their lives. The first and most courageous step often begins with asking for help and this book opens the door to expose the humanness in all of us."

-*Tina Jaeckle, Ph.D., L.C.S.W., B.C.E.T.S., F.N.C.C.M.*
Crisis and Trauma Expert, Law Enforcement and First Responders, Associate Professor and Director, Criminology, Flagler College, St. Augustine, Florida

"Karen Solomon and Jeff McGill have spent hours of intimate, personal interviews with dozens of law enforcement officers and their loved ones discussing how the day in, day out grind of policing in the 21st century, unusual traumatic critical incidents and a dysfunctional police culture slowly erodes many innocent lives.

As a thirty year veteran of this profession, I ask myself often, 'When have we as a profession become expendable?' Karen and Jeff introduce you to a dark side of law enforcement that will offer a glimpse of the physical and psychological damage suffered by dedicated servants of the shining blue shield who protect our communities. Some stories have sad endings and others are unpredictably fluid as these people attempt to rebuild shattered lives and move on in their lives. After you read this book, I hope you will advocate to your law enforcement leaders and elected officials of the serious need to invest in their law enforcement personnel's well-being by providing a balanced program of emotional first aid through preventative training and recovery to a new sense of normal."

-*Police Sergeant Mark St. Hilaire*
Metrowest area of Boston, Massachusetts

"I enjoyed reading *The Price They Pay* because the authors told stories I could relate directly to my own career. I found myself replacing the names in the book with the names of people I knew who had been through nearly identical circumstances. I felt like I wasn't alone. Even though we don't discuss these feelings face to face, I know other cops carry a similar weight with them. I guess I had always known that. But, it's nice to read and be reminded of it.

Unfortunately, these are not atypical situations. They happen over and over again across the country. Officers are forced into early retirement due to duty related injury will have a difficult time transitioning to life without police work. They shouldn't also be forced into financial ruin trying to obtain the benefits owed to them by a thankful community. These officers have been stripped of their careers trying to serve their communities. They shouldn't also be stripped of their dignity. Please share this book with your law-makers, municipal administrators, law enforcement leaders, your new cops and old. This has gone on too long. Things need to change.

Finally, thank you to the authors for putting their energy into this effort. Despite the occasional tears, *The Price They Pay* was a pleasure to read. But, more importantly, it's a noble cause. We bear a responsibility to take care of the men and women in blue, brown, and gray who take care of us."

- Steven Mueller
Dane County Sheriff's Office, Madison, WI
Traffic Team, Motor Unit, Honor Guard

THE PRICE THEY PAY

Karen Solomon and Jeffrey M. McGill

Foreword by Barry M. Thomas

Cover Design by © M. Oberkrum Designs
Edited by Michelle Perin www.thewritinghand.net
Associate Editor Keli Stubbs

This book is a work of non-fiction, some names and identifying details have been changed to protect the privacy of individuals.

Worcester, MA
www.bluehelp.org

The Price They Pay/ Karen Solomon. -- 1st ed.
ISBN 978-0-9863221-6-7
Library of Congress Control Number 2015953205

Printed in the United States of America

Contents

Foreword

Policing is hard.

When you ponder that phrase, what comes to mind? Do you agree with it? Perhaps you just find yourself not knowing what to think? My guess is several different variables impact your mindset; most notably whether you are a law enforcement officer (LEO) or if you have ever known one personally. I sometimes wonder if those who haven't walked in the shoes of a LEO can truly appreciate how difficult policing actually is – especially on the soul. My twenty-four years of experience behind the badge have told me they can't.

First things first: studies show policing is hard. At a minimum, they prove many LEO's struggle to cope with what they are exposed to. For example, research indicates that while 8.2% of the general population suffers from an active alcohol or substance abuse addiction, up to 23% of public safety personnel, including law enforcement officers, are engaged in the same struggle. Furthermore, due to the constant exposure to violence, conflict, death, pain and suffering, coupled with the extremely stressful and draining nature of their work, police run a significant risk of experiencing Post-Traumatic Stress Injuries (PTSI)/Post-Traumatic Stress Disorder (PTSD). Lastly, research by Dr. John Violanti in 2004 indicates a combination of alcohol use and

PTSD produces a tenfold increase in the risk of suicide. This small snapshot of research paints a grim picture on how policing can negatively impact those that take up its calling.

So, why does this happen? How is it that individuals brought into the profession and identified by pre-employment testing as mentally healthy, end up mired in addiction at a rate nearly three times the national average? The answer typically lies in the physical and psychological injuries officers suffer during the course of their everyday duties and the profession's internal resistance to helping its own. Whether it is a singular traumatic event or the cumulative effect of years of dealing with the physically and emotionally demanding duty – the job takes its toll and for some it becomes too much to bear. The weight of this emotional baggage is compounded by a police culture that has traditionally directed its people to suppress all emotion and go about their business, going so far in some instances to label those seeking assistance as liars, quitters or just plain weak. Is it any wonder why we've ended up with such a damaged workforce? The LEO's reading this who work in an environment that fails to support you through program or practice – you know full well what I mean. It can leave you feeling hopeless, alone and defeated.

There's also more to the equation; America's fascination with law enforcement is obvious and it contributes to the difficulties of those working in the profession. You can't turn on a television, smartphone or any other media device without being inundated with stories about the police. Riots, murders, scandals, controversies – it seems every news broadcast highlights the conflicts LEO's face on a regular basis. Unfortunately, the stories typically tend to focus on the alleged failures of police and are laced with innuendos implying wrongdoing, either in action or intent. For those of us in the profession, that is damaging. No matter how resilient you are, enduring endless scrutiny and second-guessing creates anxiety and provokes anger in LEO's which drives a wedge between those behind the badge and the communities they serve.

That's why this book is so important.

In the follow up to her award winning book *Hearts Beneath the Badge*, author Karen Solomon partnered with Jeffrey M. McGill to pen *The Price They Pay*, a raw look at the impact of policing on the people who don the uniform each day. Exposing the difficulties officers face in a professional culture that traditionally demands silence about their feelings, *The Price They Pay* is a gritty composition that gets current and former LEOs to open up about the demons they face and how they cope, or have failed to cope with a world shaped by their law enforcement profession. In an effort to humanize what many view as a superhuman profession, Solomon and McGill explore the emotional damage that is the end result of dealing with exposure to death, dismemberment, pain, suffering, conflict, fear, anger, scrutiny, vilification as well as societal and organizational pressures. Sharing stories of hope and failure gives all that have the courage to read this book a true picture of the direct and collateral damage LEO's endure each day. Solomon and McGill look beyond the uniform and put a human face on the law enforcement profession, providing the average citizen a glimpse into the hardships faced by peace officers and their families on a daily basis.

If you are a LEO reading this book, thank you. Your service, while typically minimized and underappreciated by most does not go unnoticed by all. Many, both in and outside the profession, recognize your sacrifice and commitment to bettering our communities and you are to be commended for your service – especially in light of the cost. This book is a tribute to you. The stories you are about to read will resonate deeply as they force you to face your own history and the traumatic events that have forged you into the person you are today. You will also find yourself hope-filled by the courage of many of the people highlighted. It is my prayer that those who are reading this book will be inspired knowing they are not alone in their struggles.

If you're a civilian reading this book, I thank you as well. As more members of the general public gain a deeper understanding of the psychological impact the law enforcement profession has on its people, the more compassion they will hold for these heroes. Plus, it is my hope that you become an advocate for those LEO's in your communities because they deserve the support of those they protect and serve. I applaud you for your willingness to learn.

In 2008, I was elected to sit on the Executive Board for the FBI National Academy Associates and I have spent the last seven years on that board which represents over 17,000 law enforcement members worldwide. Now, as I serve as the 2015-2016 President, I look back at how policing has changed during my tenure. The nation's mood has shifted and in this current climate of police being vilified in the media and scrutinized nationally by politicians and special interest groups, I'm not sure that LEO's have ever faced a more difficult time in our nation's history. This has to change or we're going to lose even more officers to drugs, alcohol or suicide because the job itself, as so skillfully presented by Solomon and McGill, is difficult enough when you have the support of the people – it is devastating when you don't. It is my hope *The Price They Pay* will give everyone a deeper appreciation of that.

To those whose stories are told on these pages, thank you for your courage to share. To Karen Solomon and Jeffrey M. McGill, thank you for your desire to make *The Price They Pay* a reality in order to expose the truth and lastly, to you the reader, a special thanks for your willingness to learn about the men and women that sacrifice their lives to keep others safe. You all are difference-makers in my book.

Capt. Barry M. Thomas
Chief Deputy, Story County Sheriff's Office (IA)
President, FBI National Academy Associates
2015-16

Preface

By reading this book you will enter purgatory, a place most people don't know exists. We generally see two types of police officers: the living and the dead. We honor the dead and cherish their memory. We vilify the living when they don't meet our expectations and hail them when they save our lives. What we forget are the officers that have found a resting spot somewhere between the living and the dead. Some of them still wear their uniforms and are fringe participants; others have lost the ability to wear their uniforms and are forgotten about entirely.

These are their stories. Tales of the people who have suffered enough to wish they were dead, the relatives still living in the glory created by the public for their sacrifice, the people still showing up each day in the hope tomorrow they will right a wrong that will erase their memories and the ones desperately trying to find a way to make themselves whole again.

There are officers who didn't make it into the book because they are afraid to tell their stories; they don't want their families to know what they are truly feeling and they are afraid of the ramifications if their departments found out about their struggles.

The greatest tragedy of this book is the stories not included. The information I have been trusted with and asked not to share. Many times I heard,

"Please don't tell my spouse/family/friends I have shared this with you, but it may help you understand us better." The things that are the hardest for some to say and for others to hear are the most important parts of their stories. But you won't hear them; they've been locked away in the officers' minds and now, in my heart.

While Jeff provided the intellect, I provided the emotion. We chose to give you two sides to the stories. We need people to know there are statistics to support these officers. To understand it's not just perception. Emotions aren't something they think they are experiencing; they are really happening.

We need people to understand society needs law and we, as a society, have chosen those laws. We agreed to live by those laws but we don't want anyone to enforce them. If and when they do, we want them enforced selectively. This mentality is not fair to the people who are tasked with enforcing those laws.

It's not fair that one first responder is a hero and another is a demon. It's time we find a balance; a balance both society and peace keepers can live with.

We need to realize every time a peace keeper is shot it affects every single American. Every single time an officer cannot get out of bed in the morning, it affects all of us. Because if it's happening to one officer, it's happening to others and eventually there will be no police officers left. That sounds a bit extreme doesn't it? Perhaps it's because we feel we can replace them. But who are we going to replace them with and how long will it take to train them? And, what kind of person will replace them?

If we cannot get the purest of hearts to serve and protect us, to uphold the laws we have agreed to, who will?

It's time to take a look at the men and women who are still living and walking through the shadows of darkness cast by society and find out how we can move these courageous souls out of purgatory and into a balanced reality.

Karen Solomon

Acknowledgements

This book would not have been possible without the law enforcement officers and their families contained herein. However, they are not the only ones we wish to acknowledge.

We want to acknowledge all the officers and families who have stood with us saying the weight we bear is sometimes too much.

We want to acknowledge all the officers and families who have asked for help.

We want to acknowledge all the officers and families who responded to a call for help from a peer.

We want to acknowledge all the agencies who have established stress management policies within their jurisdiction.

Finally, we want to acknowledge all the officers and families for whom we are too late to help. Too many have been lost to stress, addiction, and suicide and the time to change is now.

Jeffrey M. McGill

Part One

THE SOPHOCLES CONCEPT

He who fights with monsters might take care lest he thereby become a monster. And if you gaze for long into an abyss, the abyss gazes also into you.

- Friedrich Nietzsche

Sophocles wrote the Greek tragedy *Ajax* around the 5th century B.C. A classic tale of a man returning from war after countless battles and killing numerous enemies. After returning to the homeland, away from the battlefront, he becomes enraged slaughtering a flock of sheep, his mind believing they are real people who have wronged him. Ajax eventually realizes the grave error he has made. He has embarrassed himself and his family by his actions. Unable to overcome the shame and deal with the traumas of war, Ajax commits suicide with his own sword, leaving behind his wife and kids (Kamienski, 2013). Sophocles describes Ajax's appearance and activities following his return poignantly. While his brand of suffering has gone by many names throughout history, sadly, the outcome is similar. During the American Civil War, soldier's suffered "nostalgia." In World War I, it was renamed "a soldier's heart" and then called "shell shock" or "combat fatigue" during World War II (Kates, 1999). The cause and effect have remained the same throughout the annals of military combat. Ajax had the signs and symptoms of what is now called posttraumatic stress disorder (PTSD). The story told by Sophocles could easily be a news story today about a returning soldier from Iraq or Afghanistan, and, even today, the ending is often suicide of the combat veteran, just as in Ajax's story. While our current wars continue to bring the concept of traumatic stress to the forefront of society, the United States military members are not the only victims of this type of injury. The law enforcement community also suffers with traumatic stress, although the discussion about its existence and what should be done about it has been limited in scope.

Traumatic events are indeed nothing new, whether created by natural events or the result of some man-made action. These occurrences often haunt those who have been directly connected to the event, as well as, loved ones on the outskirts, such as coworkers, family, and friends. While devastation created by nature, such as wildfire, tornadoes, and hurricanes, can be far reaching and cause cataclysmic losses, the trauma that haunts our dreams and is the most feared is man-made. Acts of violence and depravity committed by one human being on another are personal in nature and leave those affected by them asking the questions, "Why did it happen to me?" or "Why did it have to happen at all?" With the advent of technology, the general public can view a new atrocity every day on the nightly news somewhere close to their community. The twenty-four hour news networks never seem to run short of a new act of violence to report on from across the country or the world. Despite how depraved society appears to be on the daily news, coming in direct contact with violence is still a rare event for most Americans. In the United States, the statistics show the violent crime rate to be only 386.9 per 100,000 people per year according to the Uniform Crime Report (Federal Bureau of Investigation, 2012). The crime rate has dropped from previous years and is seemingly on a steady decline. The rarity of these events protects the majority of the people from the dark side of humanity and the physical and psychological toll they take. However, law enforcement officers are an exception to this rule.

Law enforcement officers are charged with responding to, facing head on, and controlling violence for the entirety of a career, which averages 20-25 years (Paton, 2009). While the total number of violent calls an officer will deal with could vary widely depending on the area in which they work and the type of assignment they are on, it is almost certain their exposure to violent acts will be far greater than the average citizen of the United States. It is estimated that there is an almost 50% chance of a law enforcement officer being assaulted during any given year, and this alone can lead to traumatic stress injuries if not properly addressed (Kates, 1999). The head of each agency, as well as every supervisor, has a vested interest and moral obligation to prepare each officer for not only physical survival, but mental survival as well.

What happens to those who are assaulted in the line of duty? Being assaulted means you survived. Then again what does it mean to survive? Some have physical or mental injuries so traumatizing they can never pin on a badge or carry a gun again. Some try to adjust to the new normal of their lives, but are forever unable to shake the calling of being a part of the thin blue line. Most cannot come to terms with the idea their law enforcement careers are over, despite their injuries.

What happens to their family, their friends, their coworkers, and their agency? The collateral damage associated with an officer who is injured is wide spread and most often not easily managed. Initially there is support, but its quality and extent is often varied by agency preparation and commitment. Permanently injured officers may require round-the-clock care and caregivers may not only have to contend with this but also with benefits to finance this care.

In both cases, the mental strain is often more overwhelming than the physical one.

Part Two

TRAUMATIC STRESS INJURY

Once you've walked through the fire and lived, little else will burn.

- Unknown

"Shots fired! Officer Down!" The call booms across the radio. Responding units race to the scene to help their brother or sister in arms. Once the bad guy is no longer a threat, medical treatment for the injured officer becomes priority number one. When an officer suffers a life threatening physical injury in the line of duty there is a rapid sequence of events that follow. Immediate medical interventions occur to limit blood loss and ensure an open airway until EMS arrives. EMS continues care with Advanced Life Support (ALS) until definitive medical care can be reached at a trauma center. Doctors then take over and stabilize the officer and repair the physical damage. The three stage treatment, field care, evacuation care, and definitive medical attention has proven to save numerous lives who have suffered a traumatic injury.

Not unusual, no one in or out of the law enforcement community would question the need for this type of care for the physical injury. It is a process well known and used in the United States daily. Psychological injuries are just as detrimental as their physical counterparts, but not well understood in law enforcement. It is estimated that up to one third of police officers who face a traumatic event will develop some level of post-traumatic stress (Dowling F.G., 2006). Despite this high number of psychological casualties, law enforcement agencies nationwide fail to support and train for a psychological injury that can last far longer than the physical injuries received in combat (Blum, 2001).

Traumatic stress injuries can be caused by a single incident, such as an officer-involved shooting, or by the cumulative effects of a career filled with facing the worst of humanity. The piling on of traumatic events certainly takes a toll on the psyche of most officers. A retired police sergeant explained, "Your body only gets assaulted once in a while, but your brain gets assaulted everyday" (Artwohl & Christensen, 1997). Many police officers may not be trained on what to expect from their body or mind following a critical incident. The stress adds up. In addition, the method for obtaining treatment of a psychological injury, including managing its short and long-term effects, is not well advertised (Faust & Ven, 2014). If officers are aware of treatment options, they usually avoid them due to the stigma attached to seeking psychological assistance.

The need for proper psychological care is well documented and used by the military. In accordance with what is known about traumatic stress injuries courtesy of the military studies, sixty law enforcement officers interviewed following officer-involved shootings reported significant psychological effects, including disruption in regular sleep patterns, anger, and crying (Stratton, Parker, & Snibbe, 1984). These are the same psychological effects military soldiers are reporting and for which they are receiving treatment. United States law enforcement has been slow to adopt the treatment strategies developed and used by the military for these types of injuries that could mitigate the aftermath and improve recovery of officers. The military has documented that in every war it is statistically more likely for soldiers to suffer a psychological injury from combat than a physical injury, and that the cumulative effect of sixty days of combat resulted in some level of mental injury to as many as ninety-eight percent of the soldiers (Grossman & Christensen, 2008). Almost no law enforcement officer will face sixty days of continuous combat; however, a twenty plus year career has a cumulative effect that is difficult to measure. Law enforcement officers are trained to be hyper-vigilant in their surroundings because threats can be present anywhere. Being hyper-vigilant for such extended periods of time is stressful to the mind and body. This accumulation is likely to cause traumatic stress injuries and longer term psychological issues if they are not addressed when they first appear. Law enforcement involves a broad exposure to varying levels of stressful incidents that can accumulate, including incidents of violence in which the officer is an active participant, and incidents that are depressing in nature, such as child abuse investigations and suicides (Carlier, Lamberts, & Gersons, 1997). The result is that officers deal with the same mental traumas the military has already identified and for which they have established a method of intervention that leads to improved recovery.

GARY

Oftentimes, the bullied becomes the bully; the victim becomes the abuser. But, not always. After being bullied as a child because of a stutter and sexually assaulted at the age of 16, Gary chose to become the protector. *To protect and to serve.* Five words that had a deep meaning for him. Those words would be a motivating factor in his career; they would also drive him to give up the work he loved.

Gary was a believer: he believed good triumphed over evil and that the strong could prevent victimization of the weak. He also believed in change, that the actions of one could change the outcome of a situation. He believed he could harness the shame and pain of his past and put it to use helping others.

Putting those thoughts into actions didn't come easy. Initially, Gary chose to study public relations and communications in college, but he wasn't sure what direction they would take him and how he could use them to better the lives of others. At the suggestion of a friend, he took a criminal justice class and something clicked. It was then that he began to believe becoming a police officer would be the way he could give victims a voice and he could help prevent crime. His father told him finding something he loved to do was half the battle. Gary had been searching for the right career for years and it was right in front of him the whole time. Police work was everything he thought it would be, and more.

At the age of 29, Gary graduated second in his class and appeared to have a long successful career ahead of him, but little did he know he would hang up his badge after only five years of service. Gary was a good, kind man. He felt that police work should be more proactive and less reactive; he wanted to serve his community by touching people's hearts and minds so they would think twice about committing crimes. Gary is one of those people that joined the force for purely altruistic reasons. Driven by compassion not weakness, these same people seem to be hardest hit by the perils of law enforcement.

His career started off a bit slow. Although he loved the job, he found he wasn't very good at it. He'll be the first to admit it, and his Field Training Officer (FTO) will be the second. His FTO, Mark wasn't known for his patience, but he saw something in Gary he liked. He knew if he could bring him along, Gary would make a great cop. They were like-minded individuals who favored community policing in an effort to reduce crime. It took about six months before Gary was fully up to speed and was able to perform his job just as well as the other officers on his shift, some of whom had already given up on him. Looking back, Mark isn't sure if Gary would have been better off if he had given up on him as well.

Each night, Gary had a ritual: he would check the oil in his cruiser, clean out the interior, and say a prayer when he climbed in for his shift. He asked God to keep him and the people he protected safe and asked for the opportunity to help at least one person on that shift. For Gary, attitude was everything; if you went into the shift with the hope and desire to make a difference, you would.

One night he encountered a high school student who had lost his $200 tennis racket. The boy's parents had bought it as a Christmas gift and he accidentally left it on hood of his car and drove off. When he retraced his route, it was gone. A $200 tennis racket was not a small thing. It was a meaningful gift and the boy was angry with himself for not being more responsible. Sensing his despair, Gary sat down to talk to him.

"I know this isn't going to mean much to you now, and you've probably heard it before, but we all make mistakes. It's part of life and we try to learn from it. Don't waste your time beating yourself up and wondering what you could have done differently. Heck, we'd all walk around depressed if we did that."

Gary didn't leave until he felt the boy was in a better frame of mind. A few days later, the chief received a letter from the mother letting him know that Gary had taken the time to relate to her son and she was appreciative of the way Gary had provided him with a perspective that is often easier to hear when it comes from someone other than a parent. It was this kind of policing that Gary loved: helping people to understand their situation and finding an outcome with a positive aspect.

Unfortunately this scenario would be rare, as police are typically called when it's too late to change an outcome — a crime has usually already been committed. Responding to a 9-1-1 call with now Sergeant

Mark, blood noticeably marred the front door of the house. Weapons drawn, they began their room-to-room search of a normal home: pictures on the wall, books on an end table, and the smell of the night's dinner lingering in the air.

Hearing a noise, they turned to see a woman emerge from the bedroom wearing more blood than clothing. Her tear-stained face told them all they needed to know. She had been beaten and sexually assaulted. She collapsed in relief at the sight of the officers. Gary caught her, and she wouldn't let go of him until they reached the hospital. This hand in the darkness was exactly what she needed; Gary's soft southern drawl comforted her and offered her words of hope that evening. She remembered these words a year later when she contacted Gary to thank him. She had gotten help and was now safe.

Gary continued to prove himself as an empathetic officer. As Mark said, "Gary would always go the extra mile. That's what I always liked about him." Simply put, he cared. Carrying the badge is hard. Not all cops are perfect, but most of them care. There is excitement in helping someone, taking a child under your wing, or turning a bad situation around. In addition to the good feelings surrounding police work, there is necessary caution. An officer must provide protection for him or herself, and it is one that doesn't involve a Kevlar vest.

Being what is sometimes referred to as a "bleeding heart" doesn't always fit well in police work. This was especially true in a police department which was deeply entrenched in the policing styles of the 1950's and 60's, but Gary and Mark were among the new breed of police. Officers no longer needed to be six feet tall and male; women and men of many descriptions were becoming a greater part of the police force. They believed it was time to take policing in a different direction, that education and understanding mattered. Throwing people in jail was the easy part. Actually helping them was harder. Newcomers also faced the remnants of racial prejudice, and, in Gary's community, politically charged environments where a politician's child was suspected of drug dealing.

As if his perspective on policing wasn't enough to ostracize Gary, he began investigating the kids he believed were dealing drugs. This was not a popular decision among the local politicians or many members of the police force. It just wasn't the way things were done. The politicians came down hard on the department and the officers often felt the battle in the station house was greater than the one on the street. That was hard enough, but things were about to get much worse for Gary.

On December 24, 1993, Gary was called to a domestic argument. He made contact with a man named Michael, the same man that placed the 9-1-1 call. Michael had been separated from an ex-convict's sister and had gone to see his children. Unfortunately, he arrived in a drunken state and his brother-in-law didn't take kindly to his condition. He gave Michael a swift beating and sent him away.

It was now 10:30pm and, now a lieutenant, Mark knowing Gary had a knack for turning a situation around, asked Gary to drive Michael home. Gary could tell Michael was a career drinker and gently talked to him about finding help. Michael wept in the back seat while opening up about his difficult life. Gary advised him to find someone to talk to and gave Michael his name and number, just in case.

When they arrived at Michael's house, Gary opened the door and Michael left him with the words, "Officer, thank you for everything tonight. I wish you and your family a Merry Christmas." He then went inside, had more to drink, and hung himself.

Upon arriving for his shift the next day, Gary was met with suspicious eyes and pointed questions. "What did you say to him? What did you do? You were the last one to see him alive." Rather than a debriefing and discussion of the victim's past suicidal tendencies, Gary met accusations. For a man like Gary, the situation was devastating. He wondered what he could have done differently, what he could have said to save the man's life. The feeling he was put directly in Michael's path and could have somehow saved him never left Gary.

Now suffering from guilt and still investigating crimes that some didn't want investigated, work was no longer a source of joy for Gary. Politics created a division in the department and Gary had few people to confide in about his feelings about Michael's suicide and even fewer to discuss office politics with.

Despite the deteriorating conditions at work, Gary was happily married and his wife understood him and knew the value of communication in a marriage. Gary met Carmen in 1988, and their marriage had a solid foundation that would become very important as police work slowly started to tear Gary apart. As an ICU nurse, Carmen knew about stress and post-traumatic stress. She and Gary both saw things most people aren't normally exposed to. They offered each other support after long shifts and painful outcomes.

Exactly one year after Michael's suicide, the full force of police work would hit Gary squarely between the eyes and his life would never be the same. The only thing that distinguished December 23, 1994 from any other day was that the anniversary of Michael's hanging was fast approaching and it was weighing heavily on Gary's mind. The department was having a Christmas party that evening at a local bar and Gary planned to finish his shift and enjoy the party. He arrived at the stationhouse at approximately 10:10pm and was getting ready to sign out for the night.

At 10:25 a call came in. Someone's drunken uncle was harassing their family. The call went out to a female officer who was busy finishing up at an accident scene. Gary offered to take the call. It seemed like one of many calls they'd had before, so he grabbed an officer who had been with their department for just a year and headed off thinking, "We're going to have to arrest him and be late for the damn party."

As they approached the house, a 20-year-old emerged in a panic telling Gary and his temporary partner that someone had a long gun and was holding them hostage. He had run out the back door and was now in the garage. Gary called in an update to the station letting them know the situation had now escalated.

Gary and his partner made their way through the small alleyway which led to the garage, and, after ensuring there was no risk, they slowly entered. A small room with a wooden door had been built inside. The door was slightly ajar, and Gary could hear movement inside the room. While Gary was assessing the situation, a family member arrived in the alleyway beside the garage and was calling to be let in. Gary told him to stay outside, protocol for a potentially dangerous situation. Gary still hadn't laid eyes on the suspect or the weapon.

After announcing his presence, Gary slowly opened the door with his left hand. He could see a bed at the far end of the room, a man lying on it. He still didn't see a weapon. With his gun in his right hand, Gary gingerly stepped in causing the suspect to sit up suddenly and reach to his right. Gary then saw the rifle on the bed.

Suddenly, the suspect picked up the rifle. Reflexively, Gary yelled, "Drop the weapon!" beginning to back out of the room. Blood pumping in his ears, Gary watched almost in slow motion as the suspect swung the weapon toward him. He knew he was still yelling for him to drop it but he didn't hear himself. He only heard his heart pounding. He knew he could not get out of the room before a bullet reached him so he fired his gun once and retreated.

Suddenly the world appeared infinitely smaller. He was in a movie and the camera zoomed in on his life with a concave lens. In the middle of a foreign situation, he felt very alone, a situation most will never experience. He didn't see a man; he saw a rifle being pointed at him. He saw his own death if he didn't react quickly enough. He made a choice no one wants to make. He made the choice he was trained to make. No room for negotiation. No time to get out of the room. Others would have been at risk if Gary was shot. It's a lonely decision with little understanding from the people standing on the sidelines.

Gary quickly took stock of his surroundings. His partner appeared to be in shock. Family members could be heard yelling and running toward the garage. The smell of gunpowder was strong, and there was a man with a rifle either dying or still a threat a few feet away. With more caution than ever, Gary peered into the room and saw the suspect lying back on the bed, rifle still in hand pointing upward and his finger still on the trigger. Knowing he had enough time to get to the rifle before it could be brought to a shooting position, Gary rushed in, disarmed the suspect, and handcuffed him. He handed the rifle to his partner to clear the chamber.

Gary sat the suspect up and noticed the smell of alcohol. Wearing a dark green sweater, Gary didn't see any blood on him. "Oh good," he thought, "I missed. But where the hell did the bullet go?" The wall behind them was cinderblock and untouched, yet Gary saw nothing on the suspect's chest. Realizing it would have been impossible in such a small space to miss, Gary began to look more closely. He peeled back the green sweater, a t-shirt, and two more layers of clothing before he saw a little hole in the final layer. The hole was just to the left of the sternum but there was no blood on the white t-shirt. Flesh had come up through the hole of the wound blocking the flow. The suspect was bleeding internally.

Gary could see the paramedics might not make it to the scene in time to help the suspect, and, after checking vital signs, he knew there was nothing he could do to help save the man's life. He heard a cousin begging to be let in to pray for his family member. Gary knew he wasn't allowed to let someone into a crime scene. He would be breaking protocol if he did. Gary was also raised in a Baptist church and knew that it wasn't his decision to deny a man his last chance at salvation. His partner searched the cousin and Gary let him into the room to pray. Gary un-cuffed the dying man, held his left hand while the cousin held his right hand, and they prayed together. The cousin was then sent back outside, the man re-handcuffed, a pillow placed behind his head and made as comfortable as possible.

Gary turned to his partner and asked if he cleared the weapon. He then heard the words that would turn his life upside down.

"It wasn't loaded."

Gary looked at the man he had shot and asked him why he didn't just drop the gun. The man simply said, "I wouldn't have shot you." These words would echo in Gary's mind for many years. He shot a man with an empty rifle. There was no way for Gary to have known the rifle was empty. There was no way Gary could have taken the chance the man wouldn't shoot. There was now no way Gary could understand what happened that night.

Paramedics arrived and took the wounded man to the hospital where he would soon die. Gary walked out into the alley and hugged the crying cousin, said he was sorry, and began the long walk toward his cruiser. He began to operate in a fog, the same fog that surrounded him when his parents died when he was 20 and that surrounded him when he was assaulted at the age of 16. Gary believed his body was shutting down to protect him and that God shuts down the parts of you that you don't need so you can deal with things.

A crowd had now gathered outside – family and neighbors – all threatening to kill him. He was put in a cruiser where he sat for 90 minutes listening to people yell at him.

"Kill the fucking pig and his family!"

"You son of a bitch! You killed an innocent man!"

"We'll get you, you bastard!"

He scanned the crowd, seeing faces contorted in rage, waving angry fists at him. The same faces had pled for help a short time ago. The same hands that clasped his thanking him for arriving so quickly. None of them were eyewitnesses to the incident, all of them knew the suspect had a rifle, yet they all condemned him. Once Gary pulled the trigger, he condemned himself. The trauma of taking a human life would settle deep in his soul and it would take a long time to recover.

At 12:30am Gary arrived at the police station to see cruisers from multiple agencies, hallways packed with police officers chattering about the incident. When Gary stepped into the hallway, there was complete silence and everyone turned to look at him. That's when he realized what he had done. One officer hugged him and others patted him on the back while he was lead upstairs to the detective bureau.

Meanwhile, Gary's wife was working her shift at the local hospital where the victim had been brought. The words "officer-involved shooting" caused a knot to quickly form in the stomach of a police spouse. *Was it my officer? Are they okay? Why can't I get any answers!?* Panic quickly seeps in and the wait begins.

Gary wasn't answering his phone and despite multiple calls to the station, Carmen had no answers. The officers manning the phones told her Gary was coming in late from a DUI. He hadn't called Carmen because he didn't know if he was allowed to. Not knowing what he was and wasn't allowed to do after a shooting, Gary had already called an attorney, but beyond that he was lost in more ways than one.

His lieutenant offered to call his wife, but Gary refused. He didn't want her lied to and he certainly didn't want anyone else breaking the news to her. Their relationship was built on honesty and trust; he wanted to keep it that way. Despite the strength of their relationship, Gary did not want his wife involved. He didn't want her to feel what he was feeling, to know that he had shot a man. But, with a heavy heart, he finally called her.

"Honey, I just shot a man. He died but I think they brought him back but I'm not sure. I'm sorry."

"Are you okay?"

"Not a scratch."

"I know if you had to shoot someone, it was the right thing to do."

Those words were the salve Gary needed for his soul at that moment in time. He needed someone to believe in him, someone who knew that he valued human life and would not have shot someone unless forced to.

Gary spent the next few hours waiting for the state police to arrive and begin their investigation. They arrived at the same time the lieutenant received a call informing them that the victim had died. Gary's head sank into his hands; he knew his life would never be the same again. Knowing the 53-year-old man had threatened to kill himself earlier that night would offer no comfort to Gary.

There is no course at the police academy that teaches you how you will feel when you take a life. No support group waiting to welcome you into their fold and help you cope. Most departments don't even have another officer on staff that has killed someone. It's a path not well traveled, and the officers who have to take it find themselves feeling very alone. Some officers are lucky in that their department is supportive and give the officer everything he needs to find his way back. Gary didn't have that simple luxury.

Politics aren't limited to Washington—they are everywhere, and police departments have more than their fair share. In Gary's 33-man department, shootings weren't a common occurrence and yet Gary's chief didn't even get out of bed the night of the shooting to see how his troops were holding up. The chief was part of the old guard, wasn't progressive, and had already written Gary off because of his hands-on policing style and his investigation into the local politicians' kids' drug dealing. Unfortunately, he was part of what was wrong in their station and he would offer little help to Gary in the coming months; he would actually make things worse.

All too often, there is good police work but bad public relations. Gary's case was a textbook example. It was a "good" shoot, no doubt about it. The victim was suicidal and Gary had no way of knowing the gun was unloaded. The chief should have come out and publicly supported him. He should have publicly embraced Gary and his entire department. Instead, the public was left with too little information and too much speculation. There were no debriefings, no offers of emotional support, and the media was left to make their own decisions.

Three days after the shooting, Gary was back at work. Three days. Most companies offer three days bereavement when a family member dies, but is it enough when you have killed someone? Would you have slept during that time? Would you have forgiven yourself? Forgotten the face of the person who, because of you, no longer walked the earth?

Gary hadn't. In addition to the shooting, it was the anniversary of Michael's hanging. Two years, two incidents. Gary was becoming a poster child for the dark side of police work. He was also sinking into the abyss of Post-Traumatic Stress Injury (PTSI). His mind simply wasn't ready to go back to work.

His first night back on the job, Gary called his lieutenant to tell him he couldn't see. He was driving in his cruiser and suddenly went temporarily blind. This would be his first symptom of PTSI, and it was the beginning of a very long, painful road. Three months after the shooting he was feeling poorly and his mood was unpredictable. In an effort to help him, a friend read Gary a PTSI questionnaire, and Gary answered positively to 19 of the 20 questions. Confused, abandoned, lonely, and feeling betrayed, Gary denied having PTSI.

In 1994, PTSI wasn't recognized as a problem for police officers. Police were expected to do the dirty work and move on. Feelings weren't part of the job description, and Gary and many others like him became casualties of this way of thinking. There was no long term support, few debriefings, and a very distinct feeling of abandonment.

Five months after the shooting, Gary's demeanor changed drastically and he was diagnosed with clinical depression. The people closest to him began to throw up their hands in frustration and didn't know what to do for him. Gary didn't know what to do either, and he realized he was having emotional issues he could no longer control.

A man who had been willing to put his life on the line every day, who worked hard to be a good cop, Gary didn't understand why he was suddenly alone. He shot and killed a man who was going to kill him. He did nothing wrong, yet he was treated as if he had. He didn't know what was going on with himself any more than anyone else did.

Eight months after the shooting, Gary found himself sitting around his house with his gun in his mouth. He had dug himself into such a deep emotional hole he didn't know how to get out. How could an officer who should know how to handle death get to such a point? Because knowing was a myth. In reality, he *didn't* know how to handle death. Officers are simply human beings performing a service, one that happens to involve the darker side of life. They are not immune to emotional pain or depression. They function in the same ways as you or me; they live in the same garden.

Imagine this garden; one you've planted from seed, cultivated with love. When the seeds break the ground, they seek sunshine, warmth, and nutrients. The seeds have no control over the weather. They are as dependent on it as we are on our minds. You may have control over the location of your garden, the frequency with which you tend to it, and the amount of care you give it, but you can't control the weather.

It may be sunny one day, rainy the next. You prop the vines in the hopes they will flourish once the rain passes. And they may, until the next rain comes. The weather changes, sometimes without warning. Sometimes you can see it coming, much like the triggers a depressed person avoids, and you try to protect the plants before the storm. The intensity of the labor can get frustrating, especially if there is no relief in sight.

One day, a tornado or hurricane passes through. Even though you see it on the horizon, you can't stop it and you may not be able to seek shelter soon enough. The plants are torn from their roots, the garden completely destroyed. You may have thought you could protect it yourself, that the storm wouldn't be that bad, or you simply didn't know how or were afraid to ask for help. Your neighbors and family couldn't help or didn't know you needed help. The garden is gone. This is the way of depression; if you don't have it, it's very difficult to understand this cycle.

Gary's garden was beginning to wither, and, in November 1995, he would find that if he didn't make a change, he would become one of the nearly 300 police officers that commit suicide each year. Meanwhile, his wife Carmen was trying to keep their family together.

She was no longer married to the man she fell in love with. He still had the same values, foundation and heart, but he had become needy and paranoid. Carmen became the head of the household and had to manage everything. Symptoms of Gary's state of mind, including rage and hyper-vigilance, began to show in him, and Carmen and her son began to walk on egg shells. Gary never took his pain out on them. He slammed a few doors and internalized much of his pain, complicating things even more. Being a nurse, Carmen took on the role of the caretaker, which she found to be very lonely. Her family was located in another state and most people didn't understand what they were going through. They weathered the storms together, talking and seeking help. They were being held together by a slender thread, but then the thread broke.

Receiving phone calls at the station was not unusual; what was unusual was for a family member to want to apologize to the officer who killed a loved one. The woman on the other end of the line told Gary her family had called police that fateful night because they were tired of their uncle and didn't want him living there any longer. They believed if he got arrested they could get him out once and for all. In their effort to evict their uncle a few days before Christmas, they put Gary in an unthinkable position. The news was more than Gary could handle, he broke down and had to be driven home.

On November 25, 1995, a few days after the phone call and the five year anniversary of his hire, Gary was called out to the scene of domestic abuse. It was the last call of the night and, ultimately, of his career. An 18-year-old had beaten up his girlfriend, badly. He was also uncooperative and insulting toward Gary. It was Gary's last straw. He beat the young man. "If we kicked the shit out of everyone that mouthed off to us, we'd never get anything done," he said afterward. But it was more than that—Gary had reached his personal breaking point.

At the station, Gary hung up his uniform with a heavy heart and tears in his eyes; he knew he would never wear the uniform again. He had broken his oath. He became a danger to the people he swore to protect and serve, to himself and to his colleagues.

Gary had accumulated enough time to take a leave of absence, and, for the first time since the shooting, his chief talked to him. He called him on the phone and proceeded to berate him. The chief hadn't been concerned enough in the past to know that Gary was seeing a psychologist and was taking medication. Suddenly he cared — not about Gary — but about how things would look if word got out. The next day, two lieutenants were sent to Gary's house to retrieve all of the city-owned equipment Gary had been issued over the years. All this came just in time to "celebrate" the one year anniversary of the shooting.

He didn't have much time left with the department. Gary applied for workers compensation in relation to his shooting, and his claim was denied. Psychological problems, regardless of their cause, weren't covered. He needed a physical injury to qualify. As soon as the workers compensation was denied, the department took him off the payroll.

On January 29, 1996, Gary retired from the police department. There was no ceremony. No thanks for his service. Just a silent severing of his ties to the department.

Walking away from his career broke Gary's heart; it was like giving up half of himself. When he began police work, he knew it was for life. Now it was gone. Feeling lost and unsure of what to do, Gary decided to finish his bachelor's degree. On March 27th, while he was finishing school, his department approved his retirement. He was finally given permission to move on.

Gary spent the summer preparing for graduate school, but his depression still haunted him. He found himself unable to concentrate, and it became so bad that he could only read for short periods of time. Working part time jobs and going to school full time, Gary graduated two years later with a major in criminal justice and a minor in education. The two things he loved most: law enforcement and education.

Although life on the outside appeared good, internally he struggled. He had yet to find someone who could help him with his feelings, stop the nightmares, and ease his guilt. In 1998, he met another officer who had shot someone; they were able to relate to each other in a way Gary hadn't been able to relate to anyone else. They were both traveling a horrible, lonely road, but even they couldn't give each other the help they so desperately needed.

Carmen worked closely with him to try to put the pieces of their life back together; she believed in balancing the mind, body, and soul. Together they came up with a plan that would help them on the path to normalcy. What they found was they were very alone. Although each therapist took them a step further in their path, there was no local therapist equipped to treat Gary long-term. They continued to put Band-Aids on their life while seeking permanent relief.

Gary spent a lot of time traveling, trying to find the right therapist. What he found was that just because someone had a degree didn't mean they knew about trauma or PTSI first hand; it made it difficult for Gary to relate to anyone. He traveled to Montana, Miami, Boston, and San Francisco. He tried cognitive therapy, exposure therapy and more. Nothing seemed to work. Each new therapy ripped the scab off of a very raw wound, and each time it became more difficult to close the wound.

Through the years, Gary and Mark remained friends. Mark left the department shortly after the shooting because he simply couldn't handle the politics and drama any longer. He saw how Gary had been treated, had been a victim of the politics himself, and knew he too would self-destruct if he stayed. He tried many times to talk to Gary about the shooting but ended up depressed himself. It was difficult for Mark to relive, so he didn't understand why Gary shared his story with law enforcement groups. He felt it might be time to stop reliving it.

Gary wanted to stop reliving his nightmares but didn't want to stop talking about them. He believed he had much to teach, that talking about his shooting would help others. He wanted to know at least one person heard him, learned from him, and, if they found themselves in a position where they had to kill someone, they would know they were not alone. They would know what happens, what protocol to follow, and who to turn to. Gary had been alone and completely clueless about what was happening. They didn't have to be.

In 2011, Gary was still depressed, having nightmares, and continued to be lost in his own head. He had been barely coping for many years. The storms in his mind didn't want to subside and he still didn't know how to shelter himself. He joined an organization called Hunting for Heroes; they provide recreational therapy and counseling for law enforcement officers severely injured in the line of duty. Gary was concerned about participating. After all, workers compensation had already told him he wasn't injured. His emotional scars didn't count.

When he arrived for his adventure, he was quickly welcomed into the fold. A place where he thought he would never again be accepted. He found people who understood him and knew what it was like to give up the career they loved; some of them knew what it was like to have their departments turn their backs on them, and others just knew they needed each other. He felt loved and understood by his peers for the first time in a very long time. He spent the bulk of the first day in tears; he had received a wonderful gift from a wonderful organization.

In 2014, despite finding new friends and an organization he loved to be a part of, Gary still hadn't resolved his depression and PTSI. He had tried many things to stave off the ghosts. It felt good to drink because it felt good to be numb, but eventually he had to sober up. He couldn't choose what mood would strike and when. There were nightmares, agoraphobia, fear of himself, suicidal thoughts, and anger. He had been balancing these things for too long, switching back and forth between a sense of normalcy and deep despair.

The summer of 2014 found Gary awake in the middle of the night, sweating from another nightmare and feeling suicidal. He was afraid to go back to sleep again, and he knew he wasn't going to last much longer. He knew that he had to get well for his wife. She had loved him and understood him for years, and it was time to find a way to let go.

Many people say things happen only when the time is right. Perhaps Gary hadn't truly been ready for help until that night, but he finally found what he was looking for. After searching the internet for help for disabled police officers, Gary found Safe Call Now, a non-profit organization that helps first responders get the proper treatment they deserve. He spent two and a half hours on the phone sharing everything. At the end of the call, he was given the name of a therapist who specialized in rapid resolution therapy. After a three hour appointment, Gary walked out a new man.

Believe it or not, there is a moment in many people's lives when it feels as if someone has flipped a switch, that the lights have come on and everything looks clearer. Rapid resolution therapy flipped that switch for Gary. He walked out thinking, "You have got to be shitting me?! After all these years?" Gary finally found a way off medication and back into life. Not every symptom is gone. He still has issues, but it's not all-consuming the way it had been for twenty years. His biggest problem was finding out what to do with himself; he no longer needed to spend hours worrying, he was no longer exhausted, and his attitude had changed.

The first time he called Mark after the therapy, Mark knew something had changed. When they finished talking, Mark wasn't depressed. More importantly, he was no longer concerned for Gary's safety. He knew that Gary still had a long road ahead of him but that he was finally on the right path.

Gary is getting his new-found life back together and forging a new path for himself. He admits he is addicted to Copenhagen tobacco and good food. He also knows he's luckier than most. "Throughout this whole ordeal, God held my hand, gave me the strength to continue, and saved my life multiple times. Thank you Lord!"

There are many other men and women just like Gary who don't make it. They don't find the right therapist, their marriage doesn't survive, or they turn to drugs and alcohol. Just like anyone else. The biggest difference is they are misunderstood. Their trauma does not come from the same places as others. This makes it much harder to understand. Not enough of them seek help to allow a mainstream source of support. It's still a stigma for a law enforcement officer to be viewed as weak. Gary made a very important statement that put things into perspective: "My heart beats just like yours. I cry just like you. I have a family just like you. What other profession expects you to hide your emotions and humanity on and off the job? When I arrive at a car accident, do I console the mother first or cover the body of her dead child in the hope she hasn't seen it yet? What am I supposed to do with all of those memories? I need help, just like you."

STEVEN

While few officers will kill someone during their career, nearly every one of them will witness someone's death. Death is usually something most of us see sterilized. We have been notified the person has died and we view them in a funeral parlor once the bodies have been cleaned and prepped. We will experience the loss for the rest of our lives, but the presentation makes it easier. Police officers aren't notified in advance and the bodies aren't clean, but they will also experience the loss for the rest of their lives. Their loss will be in a different form, a form unique to first responders. Although there is training to help them deescalate a situation, there is no training to learn to cope with the death itself.

Steven's department sent all of their officers to Critical Incident Training (CIT), and, with just over a year on the job, he was next on the list to go. He spent a brief forty hours learning how to handle people that were suicidal or mentally ill, and forty hours learning how to save a life. Zero hours were spent learning how to cope with a lost life. Oftentimes fate deals a twisted hand, and, new out of CIT training, Steven was about to experience this.

It was just another Friday, his wife was pregnant with their second child, and he kissed his family and headed off to begin his three day weekend of twelve hour shifts. Roll call was unremarkable, the night was oddly quiet with little vehicle and foot traffic, and Steven settled in for a long, slow shift.

At approximately 10:10pm, three hours into his

shift, Steven was dispatched to "check welfare" on a distraught man. He and another officer, Ed, arrived on scene to find a man pacing around his front yard, carrying a gun.

"It's all you, you had CIT training," Ed said to Steven.

Steven quickly looked around and noted the nicely restored 1988 Dodge pickup parked in the driveway and the fact that the nervous man had a tight grip on his gun. Steven and his partner had no choice but to un-holster their weapons.

Addressing the man, Steven said, "I'm Officer Jones from the police department, I just want to see if you're okay."

"No, I'm not alright," he replied.

As he sought shelter behind the truck, Steven remembered the suicide by cop videos he had seen in the academy and hoped this night would not turn into a case study. He didn't want to kill anyone and he certainly didn't want to see his fellow officers forced to do so. He immediately opened the dialogue with the distraught man.

"Why do you want to do this?" Steven asked.

"I'm broke and my wife left me. I have nothing left to live for, nothing," replied the man.

Steven kept talking. They talked about high school, college, marriage, and baseball. They were both Royals fans and at the time the Royals were fifteen games out of first place.

While Steven continued to talk, two other officers had arrived on the scene, his sergeant and another officer, Bill. Ed was "a sneaky, ninja, SEAL

Team Six kind of guy who could sneak up on anyone," and, when he and Steven arrived, he had
positioned himself at the corner of the house and the
man never knew Ed was there. Bill stood in a neighbor's yard behind a tree and the sergeant positioned
herself behind a nearby house with a long gun.

For three hours, Steven and the man talked. During those three hours, a mistake was made. Whether
or not it would have changed or accelerated the outcome, no one can say. The sergeant was young and
inexperienced. She did not call for back up, a nego-
tiator, or the SWAT team. She was the highest
ranking person on shift that night.

As the night progressed, Steven's arms were getting tired. He was standing behind the truck, his
arms outstretched, aiming his weapon at the man. At
one point, the man put his gun on the hood of the
truck but there was no way for the officer on scene
to safely reach him and get him into custody. His behavior was too erratic and his gun was kept too
close. Eventually, the memory of the patrol car's
dash cam would fill up and stop recording.

Not knowing what else he should be doing and
hoping assistance was on the way, Steven continued
to try to talk the man into getting help, and, for a
moment, he thought he'd broken through. What Steven thought was a sign of clarity for the man, that
suicide wasn't the way out, was actually something
entirely different. The man stopped pacing, looked
at Steven and said, "You are trying really hard. You
are doing a great job. This isn't on you."

As the man brought the gun to his mouth, Steven
began yelling, "Stop! Stop! Stop!"

He didn't acknowledge Steven; he put his gun in his mouth and pulled the trigger.

"Fuck!" was the only reaction Steven could muster. It wasn't supposed to go down that way. He was supposed to be able to save the man's life. He was trained to talk him out of pulling the trigger. He didn't understand what he was supposed to do when he failed.

The sergeant finally called the captain of patrol, the major, and the detective sergeant for assistance. Within fifteen minutes they were surrounded by a team of people whose support Steven had badly needed three hours earlier.

The captain of patrol, an Iraqi war veteran, assured Steven it wasn't his fault. That was the sum total of his debriefing. His gun was replaced, he went to the station to complete his report and two hours later he was back on the road. Over the next three hours, he answered an alarm call and a trespassing call. He finished his shift at 7am as though it was a routine evening.

Steven received no time off; he was back to work the next day. On Sunday night, he and a few co-workers split a six pack of beer and talked about how shitty the weekend had been. But his mind never quite made it back. In the days immediately following the incident, Steven didn't talk about it, not even to his wife. When he slept, he had nightmares. He became restless and irritable and his wife noticed the change in him. One month after the incident, his wife sat him down, told him he was being an asshole, and, with a new baby on the way, they needed to fix it. Steven finally told her what happened.

"She handled it like a champ," Steven said. "I have a really hard time with my feelings but she was able to help me through it. She knew what I needed most when I needed it."

Steven still hadn't learned that having a supportive spouse wasn't all he needed to survive emotionally. He had yet to see a professional. Steven worked for a very young department, many of his peers were fresh out of the academy and didn't believe in therapy or talking to each other about their pain. Their unspoken motto was, "Great job, now move along. You've got more work to do." It's a theme all too common in law enforcement. Steven moved along, coped as well as he could, and kept working.

A few months later, his son was born and he began a year that nearly broke him. He celebrated his first day back on the job after the birth by responding to a call where a little girl had been pushed down the stairs. Steven performed CPR until the paramedics arrived. She had been pronounced dead because her brain had swollen so much but, "By God's grace and a clever surgeon, she made a complete recovery." Steven spent his time talking to the sister of the victim, and he was able to find out she was being sexually abused by the mother's boyfriend and he had pushed her down the stairs. She was 7-years-old.

The next call Steven remembers was a hit and run. He was the first to arrive on scene to find another young girl. The girl's head had been crushed by the weight of a Hummer. The next call — a shooting. Another young girl, shot through the shoulder. One after the other, dead and injured. Steven's psyche was being assaulted with sights and sounds that would begin to chip away at his carefully formed emotional defenses. He sought no help and none was offered.

The next significant incident would change Steven forever: an apartment building fire. Steven and another officer arrived to the sounds of the screams of parents desperately trying to find their children. They ran inside believing there were three children trapped; they scooped them up and ran outside with a feeling of elation and relief. They had saved the children from certain death. The feeling was short lived. A frantic mother approached them, "Where's my daughter?"

Steven and the other officer tried to re-enter the building but the fire had become too intense. All they could do was watch in horror as a partial wall of the building collapsed, revealing the child's location. They could see and hear her, but they couldn't save her. Her screams were mixed with the screams of her mother. Eventually her screams were silenced and she was no longer visible. Her mother continued to wail in pain, others dropped to their knees and sobbed while the first responders choked back their own tears and finished their jobs, the emotion overwhelming. Every person on the scene was altered that day. A piece of every one of them became part of the ashes.

Once again, they filled out their reports and went back to work, little soldiers marching to a seemingly endless tune of despair. The lack of support led the other responding officer to become an alcoholic, and it wasn't until his suicidal threats made their way up the chain of command that someone realized the officers needed psychological help. Every first responder on the scene was required to attend one counseling session. One. To quiet the screams they heard in their sleep. Steven believed he could handle it. He was made to believe he could handle it. He was a cop; it was part of the job. He became another undiagnosed case of PTSI.

He was also a husband and a father, but he stopped caring about what was going on at home. Despite his great love for his wife and children, he distanced himself from them and didn't know how to make his way back. Once again, his wife sat him down and told him they needed to figure out ways for him to cope or he would find himself alone.

Steven learned, as most cops do, that it was his problem, not the department's. Once his one mandatory counseling session was complete, he was expected to return to work as good as new. He enrolled himself in four months of therapy and worked to make himself as close to good as he could.

Today he lives with the memories and the scars; Steven will always have PTSI. Fire scenes make him nervous, even on television, and he loses sleep on the anniversary of the suicide and the fire. His subconscious will never let him forget. Neither will his commendations. He received a Meritorious Award for the little girl pushed down the stairs and a Life-Saving Award for the children that made it out of the fire. They are haunting reminders of the emotional perils of his job, of the things he has seen and will continue to see. Rewards for the heinous acts of other people.

Part Three

TRAUMA MEDICINE FOR THE MIND

*When I stand before thee at the day's end, thou shalt
see my scars and know that I had my wounds and also my
healing.*

- Rabindranath Tagore

The clearly established protocols to address
physical injuries save countless lives each year. The
medical community has refined their operation with
9-1-1, rapid intervention, and rapid transport to provide trauma patients with the best chance at survival
and long term recovery.

Just as there is an accepted medical plan to manage traumatic physical injury, the same type of
program has been developed to manage psychological traumatic stress injuries. The prognosis for an
officer with a traumatic physical injury is improved
by early intervention due to personnel who are increasingly more skilled during each step in the
process. The same situation applies to psychological
injuries. Officers who receive the best psychological
care the soonest are those who have the greatest

long-term improvements (Artwohl & Christensen, 1997). Immediate intervention at the scene is vital, followed by more advanced care to ensure stability and to determine the next phase of appropriate assistance. Then finally, definitive care to put things back in order to manage the long-term effects of psychological injuries.

Officers facing a traumatic stress injury resulting from a single incident, or officers reaching a breaking point from cumulative strain are in desperate need of some basic psychological first aid. This initial intervention commonly falls to the first responding unit or supervisor to arrive and find an officer in need. Nationwide most law enforcement officers lack the understanding to provide traumatic field care for psychological injury. While officers are trained with multiple options on how to deal with members of the public who have been traumatized as the victim of a crime, those in law enforcement rarely discuss how to take care of each other. The goal of the immediate response is to limit the chances of a temporary injury becoming a longer lasting wound in need of more serious care. On-scene psychological intervention is consistent with the model used when initially dealing with a physical injury, such as a gunshot wound in the field. One-on-one intervention should last no more than a half hour and result in the officer being assured his/her physical and mental responses are normal and they are not alone (Kates, 1999). This initial intervention will be rudimentary in nature, but, if handled properly, it sets the groundwork for all future interventions.

The second phase of treatment for medical trauma is the response and interventions used by paramedics to establish short term stability. The paramedics also make an assessment to determine the need of additional treatment. In response to the mental trauma, the same type of assistance and assessment is required from advanced trained personnel to mitigate long-term effects and address short term issues. This is commonly provided by peer support programs and critical incident stress debriefings. While fancy words have been used to describe these discussions, they are not much different from the evening debriefings that occurred in the years prior to the 24/7 combat abilities we see with today's military. During early wars, combat occurred during the day, then at night warriors would return to the camp fire to eat and discuss their actions with fellow warriors who would listen and empathize (Grossman & Christensen, 2008). Critical incident debriefing teams are made up of trained peer supporters who share a common background with the traumatized officer. These peer supporters are prepared to move an individual or group of people through a step-by-step process allowing the participants to tell their story and make connections with other's stories. These debriefings are organized discussions that take the participants mentally back to the time of the traumatic event and allow them to talk their way through their physical and emotional responses. The benefits of a critical incident debriefing are those who attend find a connection between their perspectives, can fill in gaps in memory, and can support each other. The goal of a debriefing is to allow the participants to move incrementally through the critical incident and release strong emotions that may be suppressed (Kates, 1999).

Studies have shown that line officers, who are often reluctant to seek psychological help, are willing to discuss issues with trained peer support teams (Dowling F.G., 2006). Just as there is a time constraint for the effectiveness when dealing with traumatic hemorrhaging from a gunshot wound, there is a time frame where critical incident debriefings and peer support are the most effective. These types of interventions are most successful within the first 24 to 72 hours after a traumatic event (Mitchell & Everly Jr., 1996). Peer support helps the injured officers learn what is likely to occur to them physically and mentally in the immediate future, what to do to mitigate the effects, and what to do if these effects do not begin to subside over the next coming weeks. These debriefings act as a conscious shift of thought processes about the critical incident and try to separate the emotional response from the cognitive response (Blum, 2001). The officer can take back control over their emotions and flashbacks that may be interfering with their lives, and they are forced to admit that they do not have total control over all situations. They also allow for the group of people involved in the critical incident to share their feelings of guilt (Grossman & Christensen, 2008)and support each other throughout the process and help each other get on the path toward recovery. In addition, these debriefings can be used to educate family members of the normal reactions that may occur in the officers as their minds recover from a traumatic incident (Artwohl & Christensen, 1997). Peer support groups are especially beneficial to law enforcement officers who are notoriously distrustful of people who are outside the law enforcement world. Peer support members bring a level of credibility that cannot be achieved by regular psychological interventions conducted by the best doctors because peer supporters have a direct connection within the career field (Mitchell & Everly Jr., 1996). The law enforcement community is unique in its training, day-to-day interactions, constant pressure, and distrust of the general public. The resistance to seeking mental health treatment due to the stigma associated with it may mean the only help an injured officer may find is from a peer supporter. If help is sought from a peer supporter, an opportunity is automatically created to assist the officer in obtaining further assistance to deal with the long-term psychological damage if needed.

Finally, the third phase of treatment for mental trauma is professional psychological care. Peer support is not counseling and cannot resolve long-term post-traumatic stress disorder. Psychologists have gained a tremendous amount of knowledge about traumatic injuries over the last decade of military combat in Iraq and Afghanistan (Grossman & Christensen, 2008). The large number of psychological casualties as a result of military combat in the relatively short amount of time has resulted in the development of new techniques to assist in repairing the significant damage caused by the traumatic stress injury much like the trauma surgeon dealing with physical injuries. Professional counseling addresses the long-term issues associated with the traumatic stress injuries that are too challenging for initial responders or peer support groups. The majority of officers will not need this level of care and may find that after a critical incident debriefing they begin to improve rapidly. But, for those who do need psychological care, this will likely result in some benefit.

MICHAEL

Oreo cookies. What kind of memory does that evoke for you? Milk? Something delicious? Fun? Oreos should have a relatively benign emotional effect on people, not trigger nightmares or panic attacks. Unless you were eating them the night your life changed.

Joe and Michael had worked together for four years, but had been on the same team for only eight months. They were both divorced, had kids, and loved their jobs. There was nothing unusual about either of them.

Joe loved being a cop, training new cops, and looking for ways to make the job easier and better. Helping to improve technology at his department was not unusual or noteworthy to him; he was just doing his job. He had worked an FBI task force, had a vast amount of knowledge, was well-respected, and, "could talk just about anyone into handcuffs."

If Joe had a problem with you, he'd let you know and hold you accountable. He had little patience for incompetence. As serious as he was about his work, he also liked to have a little fun on the job. Make a mistake on the radio? You were fair game for Joe's bloopers. He'd get a copy of the recording from dispatch and play it for you when you least expected it or it would be your ringtone on his phone until the joke wore thin.

He loved his kids, and if he wasn't working he was with them. He wanted the best for them and was willing to do whatever it took to be there for them and ensure their happiness. His children were his first love, his job his second, and food his third. Joe loved to eat. Saturday mornings were reserved for breakfast at the Bear E Patch. People there knew and loved him. He was as much a fixture as the oven in the kitchen. Joe and Michael would have breakfast there on Saturdays as long as they were partners.

Joe was easy to work with, quick to help, and honest about what he saw in other officers. Michael was unloading a suspect at the station when the prisoner's shoe got caught on the lower portion of the seat in the police car. Michael told the man to push himself up so he could pull his foot out, but the man refused. After some back and forth, Michael gave in, leaned down to release the man's foot and the man spit in Michael's face. So angry he was shaking, Michael had the man sit on the ground until the tactical team arrived for booking. When they arrived, they wouldn't take him. The man said he was injured and needed to go to the hospital. It was Michael's responsibility to take him but he was so angry he thought someone else should do it. Joe arrived on scene with a trainee, assessed the situation, and asked Michael, "What are you going to do when you are a supervisor? You've got to get your emotions under control." Joe wasn't angry, rude or judgmental; he was simply matter of fact.

Michael also loved his daughter, his job, and food. Michael was raising a daughter with Down's syndrome; Sara was the reason Michael got up in the morning. His biggest concern was how much she would develop emotionally and physically and whether or not he'd be there to help her.

Michael, like Joe, loved training. Michael had been a teacher before he became a police officer. He wanted to teach poor children, help them and have an effect on their lives. He taught on a Navajo reservation, but because most families lived below the poverty line with no water or electricity and too much domestic violence, Michael found teaching difficult. He hated that he was providing students with a safe and happy environment for about 6-8 hours a day but couldn't do anything once they left the school. He saw law enforcement as a way to impact their lives on a wider scale — not just in the classroom.

Michael had always been driven toward altruistic pursuits. Along with his teaching stint, he served his country and worked with sexually abused children before he settled on law enforcement in 2004.

Joe and Michael found themselves on a rare team. Michael felt they "got along really well and complimented each other's weaknesses. Teams that mesh so well don't come along that often; we really enjoyed working together. It was just a really nice group to be around and to work with."

The team Michael and Joe were assigned to work day shift for 28 days then switched to night shift for 28 days. They worked 12 hour shifts, six to six. Each month when they arrived for their first shift back on nights, they would have an Oreo cookie party. Everyone brought their favorite flavor and they would enjoy the cookies before they began the long month of nights. Michael loved the mini-Oreos hand dipped in chocolate that could be picked up at the candy shop on the Market, while Joe's favorite was the root beer float flavor. On September 8, 2014, the Oreo party was held in Joe's honor because he had served the most warrants in the previous month.

Both men arrived at the station after a normal day. Both in jovial moods, they expected Monday to be relatively easy. Joe joked that if he had to run someone down that evening he would probably puke Oreos. Joe had a trainee 5 weeks out of the academy with him that evening. Michael had finished with his trainee three weeks prior and hadn't been assigned a new one yet.

They began taking calls at 6:45pm.

A few miles away at an apartment complex, Michael Oswald was drunk and pounding on a neighbor's car. Two Charleston County deputies lived in that same complex, and they walked over to see what was going on. Oswald shut himself in his apartment, yelling to the off-duty officers that he wasn't coming out. Because the tension between Oswald and his neighbors had been escalating for forty-eight hours, uniformed officers were called in.

Joe, his trainee, Michael, and another deputy were in the area; Michael was the last to arrive on the scene. Oswald had been videotaped pounding on a car and he didn't appear to be settling down anytime soon. Joe and the first deputy on scene decided they would charge Oswald with disorderly conduct. This would keep him locked up for 24 hours and give the owners of the car, a young couple a few doors down, a break while they decided how to move forward.

Oswald liked to get drunk and get kicked out of bars, but the officers didn't suspect he would be violent. "There was nothing to give us any indication, no gut feelings, nothing. We had over 50 years of experience between the four of us," Michael said.

Oswald lived in a second floor apartment next to a center staircase. There were two other staircases on the building—one on each end. He refused to come out of his apartment, so Joe and Michael settled near the middle staircase to wait. Police called the apartment manager for assistance and the officers were told it would be thirty minutes before he arrived. They waited.

While they waited, they talked about their families, what they would be doing off duty that week, and Oreos. Just four guys talking, waiting for access to an apartment.

When the apartment manager arrived, the fourth deputy went around to the back of the building in case Oswald decided to jump off the back balcony and run. Joe took the key from the manager. To the left of the door was a small window. To the right was a larger double window. Joe stood to the left of the door. The deputy that lived in the apartment complex was now standing behind Joe to his left and Michael stood two feet to Joe's left with the trainee, behind him to the right. The other officer that lived in the building stood behind the trainee with the apartment manager forty feet behind him.

Joe announced their presence again, put the key in the door and opened it a few inches. A latch lock didn't allow them to open the door any further and, unbeknownst to them at the time, Oswald had wedged his bed against the door. Joe leaned in a bit and said, "Michael, we need you to come outside."

Oswald answered, "Who is it?"

"Charleston County Sheriff's office. We need you to come outside."

Oswald answered in a calm, but unintelligible voice and began shooting.

Joe was shot in the head and killed instantly. Additional shots hit Joe's radio, taser, and his torso, spinning his 6'3" frame around. Shooting with an AK-47, Oswald's bullets ripped through Joe's body armor.

Startled, Michael looked directly at Joe as he was hit.

"I watched the life leave Joe's body, saw his hands relax as he fell."

Everyone was falling for cover.

"He was very meticulous in his shooting. He was walking his rounds through the wall and keeping rounds low because he figured we were going to drop for cover. It was like he was hunting us. In literally one second Joe was down and 7 or 8 more rounds were fired off," Michael recalled emotionally. "I may have tried to do some weird ass river dance trying to get around the bullets. It worked. They didn't hit me. I have no recollection of popping the thumb break or pulling my weapon out. The first memory of my weapon was sighting it and squeezing rounds off through the window. I felt a pain in my right leg but I wasn't worried because I had broken my leg in three places while I was in the Marines. That hurt more than the bullet. I tried to step backward out of the way and my right leg collapsed sending me onto my back. I had a hole in my tibia."

Oswald stopped firing just long enough for Michael to call out for help. The rookie helped Michael pull himself back from the door a bit but he was still in the breezeway with Joe's body. Still in the line of fire. He looked at his leg and "was pissed at myself for being a pussy while Joe was down. It was just a small bullet hole." Michael tried to get up twice but couldn't; his leg was too weak.

Oswald started firing again. So did Michael. He knew he had to keep Oswald inside the apartment. If he made it outside, they'd all be dead. He knew whatever weapon Oswald had was very powerful and he needed to stay inside until help arrived. Michael heard one more shot and then silence. It had been less than two minutes since the first shot. Not knowing what to expect, Michael reloaded.

A sergeant with the Charleston Police Department made his way to Michael's side and tried to evacuate him, but Michael wouldn't budge. Although he can't remember what happened, he was told that he vehemently argued that he wasn't going anywhere. Michael does remember a SWAT officer named Eddie sitting next to him with his rifle assuring Michael that he would cover the scene. Although Michael agreed to leave, it took a little more convincing to get him to holster his weapon so he could be loaded into the ambulance and taken to the hospital. In shock and afraid, he wanted to protect himself and his friends. He was lost in the horror.

While he was en route to the hospital, Michael was very concerned about his mother. She lived nearby and he was afraid she would see the shooting on the news. He gave her phone number to every person he passed hoping someone would reach her in time. He also worried about Joe's parents. Who would tell them?

Joe was put in the trauma bay next to Michael's. He had no chance, but the doctors did everything they could. The trauma doctor hugged Michael and apologized. "I tear up every time I think about it. Because, just like cops, doctors aren't supposed to show emotion. But that doctor came over and shared his emotion with me. He shared a very special moment with me." Michael was wheeled to Joe's side to say goodbye.

Michael also requested a rabbi be available for his mother when she arrived. Even though he was forty-five years old, he was still her baby. She was going to have a difficult time accepting what had happened and seeing Michael as a cop. Until then, he had tried to keep the dangers of his job away from her.

In addition to seeing the dangers of the situation, Michael's mom was introduced to his colorful language. Michael had two choices: the doctors could perform surgery or allow his leg to heal naturally in a cast. "Doc, I'm a fucking cop. If you have a legal question, I'm your guy. But when it comes to medical shit, that's what you're for. I want to get back to work as soon as fucking possible. Get me back to full-fucking duty ASAP."

While the doctors planned to set Michael's leg, his mother went out of his room and hugged every single officer that lined the hallways. That night she learned what it meant to be supported and loved by law enforcement. She learned that they would stand by her as long as she needed. It helped her get through that night and the days to come.

Michael spent six days in the hospital; he's lucky he didn't lose his leg, even luckier he didn't lose his life. Narcotics, adrenaline, and disbelief carried Michael through the first 24 hours. The support from his agency carried him through the rest; they kept him distracted, kept him from his thoughts. "Their strength that night was unimaginable. They all knew Joe, they were hurting badly, but they made themselves available for me. Two guys sat in my room and cracked ridiculously inappropriate jokes just to make me laugh."

Michael had visitors non-stop in the hospital, and they kept him from focusing on what had happened. If he didn't have visitors, he had thousands of calls and messages from well-wishers. Everyone wanted to be his friend on social media. People from all over the country were reaching out to him, and Michael tried to respond to everyone. He felt that if they had taken the time to reach out to him, he should respond. It began to take a toll. He wasn't spending enough time on himself, or with his mother. One afternoon, when things had quieted down, she sat next to him and said, "You know Michael, this is the first time I've had the chance to sit alone with you." He was so busy avoiding reality he had avoided his own mom.

Two days after being discharged from the hospital he attended Joe's funeral in a wheelchair. It was more emotional than Michael ever would have imagined. When he arrived home, alone with his thoughts, he began to realize the magnitude of what happened. He wouldn't fully accept Joe was dead until eight months later on Joe's birthday.

It took three months before Michael could sleep for more than an hour at a time. Acceptance and understanding were slow to come. Without protocol in place to assist him, Michael coped alone with the violence he witnessed: Joe's death and the fact he could have easily died as well. All too soon he would have to bear yet another burden—he had taken someone's life.

Two months after the shooting, Michael learned Oswald didn't kill himself. He was killed by Michael. During the first round of shots, Oswald had positioned himself in such a way that the officers' fire would never have reached him. When he began the second round of shots, he had moved behind the door and was no longer behind cover. He was doing exactly what Michael feared he would do: he was trying to make his way outside.

Michael never saw Oswald; he just kept shooting. The first bullet struck Oswald in the lower abdomen, at which time he bent over and the second round entered through his left clavicle, made its way through major organs, and exited the right side. Oswald walked around the bed, collapsed against the wall leaving a bloody handprint and dropped his weapon which fired into the wall when it hit the ground.

Oswald had over a thousand rounds of ammunition in the apartment and was planning to kill a lot more people. Initially, Michael felt a sense of pride and relief that he had avenged Joe's death and stopped Oswald from killing anyone else. That feeling immediately gave way to a discomfort that still lingers. Michael believes only God should take a life. It's a paradox difficult for a police officer to reconcile. In less than two minutes, Michael watched a life be taken and took one himself.

What's even harder for Michael is to see the pain Joe's parents are in. Michael and Joe have been honored over and over again, and it's heartbreaking to see them relive that night each time they accept a posthumous award.

Through all of this, Michael recognized he needed mental help to recover from the shooting and he wasn't afraid to ask for it. The more he was left alone, the more his mental state deteriorated. Initially he sought help through his department's Employee Assistance Program (EAP). Sent to a therapist that "went through a checklist," he explained, "she wasn't really helping me. She wasn't equipped for my situation." Michael needed someone specifically trained to handle law enforcement PTSI, and, after a few dead ends, his attorney told him about Dr. Greg Dwyer. A Forensic Psychiatrist, Dr. Dwyer specialized in first responder PTSI.

The workers compensation case manager logged Dr. Dwyer's information and Michael made an appointment. The day before Michael's appointment, his case manager told him he needed to get third party administrator approval. Michael spent the day leaving messages for everyone because he was unable to get a live person who could help. Four days after Michael attended his first counseling session, his phone call was finally returned. His claim was denied. His attorney could not refer him to a doctor. Michael explained his attorney wasn't referring him to a doctor. He told them his attorney knew a specialist who handled cases like his and suggested he make an appointment. Michael was told he needed a prescription from a doctor to see a specialist, not a suggestion from an attorney.

After spending hours on the phone, Michael's frustration mounted because he wasn't getting the proper information or help. He was told, "We don't train our case manager on the steps for mental health because it happens so infrequently."

Michael began to make even more phone calls. He thought it was simply a training issue and his claim would be approved. Workers compensation told him they don't provide mental health assistance training to their employees "because law doesn't require us to. You want to change it, change the law." It wasn't just a training issue. His claim had been denied.

Michael wanted help; he wanted people to be able to file a claim properly the first time and get the help that they needed without confusion. It wouldn't take long before his confusion turned to outright anger. Now that Michael's claim was on file, he was told because South Carolina is a non-union state they don't recognize PTSI as a workers comp claim for first responders. Every other employee in the state can claim PTSI when filing for workers compensation, but not the ones that seem to need it most.

PTSI benefits are not something a rookie would think to look for when they start their new career and it's not common knowledge that many states don't cover it under their healthcare plan. Unknown to the men and women of South Carolina, Section 41-1-160, Code of Laws of South Carolina prohibits first responders from receiving workers compensation for mental trauma. Like Michael, they find out too late. He wouldn't accept that and decided to change things, pursuing coverage for all first responders via South Carolina Bill S429. Bill S429 passed the Senate subcommittee 5-0. Now it's sitting stagnant on the Senate floor blocked by people who don't want to pay. The organization of municipalities and counties don't want to pay for mental health care of first responders in South Carolina. Michael continues to fight. He travels to conferences speaking about his incident and the list of challenges he has faced since. Receiving mental health care is at the top of that list.

Michael's not the only one suffering. He wasn't Joe's best friend; he was simply standing two feet away when Joe died. Other people on the team were closer to Joe and they are still struggling but won't admit it openly. They're trying to do it the old-fashioned cop way by brushing it aside. People who have vacationed with Joe or expected him to be at their significant life events have cancelled or refuse to make plans because they can't do it without him. Not yet.

Carrying memories and emotions in a profession where those two things can make or break you is confusing. Michael feels guilty for developing PTSI. He wonders why he isn't as strong as everyone else, wonders why he is the only one struggling openly and whether or not anyone understands or cares about what he is experiencing. He says, "It's very *Patton*-esque. There is a scene in the movie *Patton* where he sends the guy with PTSI right back into the field. That's what it's like." Joe was shot and killed in front of his co-workers, Michael was shot, and all of them were targets. Michael and his squad were given a week off to grieve, but others, who were close to Joe and present at the scene, were sent back out on the streets like a child whose parent slaps a Band-Aid on a scrape and sends them back to the playground.

Michael is proactively working to rid himself of all of those feelings and get back to work. He isn't guided by policy. He knows he has to heal mentally as well as physically to truly perform his job again. His gear from that night is still in evidence; he can't pick it up until he is ready to go back to work. When he is, his psychiatrist will accompany him to get it. He also plans to simulate the evening of the shooting. The North Carolina Highway Patrol helps officers who have been in critical incidents by rebuilding the scenes and simulating incidents repeatedly until the officers can make it through. He's also asked to be assigned to a Field Training Officer for a few weeks so he can ease back into the job and make sure he can do what he needs to do. This is his biggest obstacle. He is truly concerned about his reaction when he gets back on the streets. He knows the daily observation reports are the key to him being able to remain on the job. He needs to assure himself he is fit for duty.

Michael is soft-spoken, self-aware, and guarded. What's apparent to everyone, though, is that he still loves his daughter more than anything. He sometimes wonders if his love for Sara has contributed to his PTSI. He constantly worries about what will happen to her after he is gone. No matter how long Michael lives, Sara will live longer. Not knowing what will become of her scares him. He tries to focus on enjoying every moment with her.

"Seeing those bullets coming at me knowing at that moment I almost left Sara without a dad...she would never have been able to understand/comprehend it. My mortality as a father has played a huge role in what I have been going through. From September to January, Sara couldn't stay with me. It was the first time in her life she hasn't been able to be with me. She wasn't potty trained and I couldn't lift her to put her on the potty or in the car or chase after her. For four and a half long months I only saw her for short periods of time when my mom brought her over. It was rough on both of us and Sara couldn't understand what was going on. She just knew daddy had a 'boo boo.'

"She began acting out in school because she wasn't able to communicate her confusion. She couldn't see me as much as usual. It broke my heart. That was a lot of the sadness and despair that almost left her without a father.

"I had been planning to do the Buddy Walk with Sara, a Down's syndrome fundraiser, but I was still in a wheelchair and couldn't do it. I put out a message on Facebook asking for help because I wanted someone to walk with Sara, and over 100 first responders showed up to support Sara. For the first time ever, I saw Sara realize that there were people there for her. She understood they were there for her. It was a tremendous thing to witness your child understand that all these people care about her. That meant more to me than anything.

"The first night she was able to stay overnight I was so happy; it was as if everything was right with the world again. She has taught me so much about life and love, the importance of the smallest success and milestone. She's given me that gift. I am very blessed to have her give that to me."

Most days Michael feels like he's stuck; he's reminded of the incident every day because of the pain in his leg. He doesn't feel left behind, but he feels like everyone else has been able to move on. Everyone is still very supportive, no one begrudges his recovery, and they are very supportive of his plan to return to work and not just throw him back in a patrol car.

While Michael fights to become physically prepared to go back to work, he is also fighting to become emotionally fit. Many other officers return to work physically prepared, but not emotionally. Because of the lack of resources and protocol, there is little chance that they will receive the intervention they need at the time it's needed.

Part Four

AGENCY POLICY

The price one pays for pursuing any profession, or calling, is an intimate knowledge of its ugly side.

- James Baldwin

The death of an officer is a terrible tragedy for an agency, but it is a known risk that each and every officer accepts the day they take an oath and pin on their badge. Law enforcement death notifications are usually delivered to the family in person by a supervisor. Law enforcement tradition often dictates the events following a line of duty death (LODD) and unfortunately too many agencies are becoming proficient at burying one of their own. Ceremonial customs, a sea of uniforms, the posthumous awarding of Medals of Valor and the playing of *Taps* all serve to bring closure to a line of duty death. Following the burial, the family receives life insurance and other benefits from local, state, and national organizations as an attempt to ensure the family is taken care of and for society to pay its debt to an officer who has paid the ultimate sacrifice in defense of them.

The waters become muddy when we begin to look at agency policy addressing officers who are severely injured in the line of duty but survive. Many agencies have no policy addressing the most basic tasks when it comes to managing this process. Notifications of line of duty injuries have occurred over the phone or by officers who have limited knowledge of the extent of the injury or the current status of the officer. Family members have driven themselves to the hospital or worse yet to the scene. Injured officers are notified by human resources via mail or phone call that they are being retired without warning or ceremony. Officers are often required to hire an attorney to fight for benefits that would have been awarded if they had been killed.

How can we bring healing and closure to an officer who is a living reminder of our vulnerability? Have officers who are no longer capable of returning to work due to line of duty actions not paid a high enough price to earn the pomp and circumstance that comes with a ceremonial retirement? Are they not deserving of benefits to ensure they and their family are taken care of? Does your agency have a policy? It should.

DAN

When you think of a disabled police officer, what is your first thought? Do you wonder how he was injured, how his family is coping, or if he has everything he needs? Do you think of his years of service and wonder if the city leaders are supporting him? Or do you wonder how much he is costing the taxpayers or if he's really hurt? Sadly, too many people wonder the latter. What's worse is that some cities wonder the same thing.

Dan and Wendy learned the hard way that it's very difficult to get benefits for an officer injured in the line of duty. Finding help becomes an uphill battle: lawsuits, legislation, and pleading become a routine part of their lives. Some locales are downright hostile to the injured officer. They don't want the money for the officer's care to come out of their pockets. Dan and Wendy's battle for federal benefits started seven years ago.

Dan's commitment to his community was seamless. He had no reason to believe their commitment to him would be anything but reciprocal. Dan's family has carried a professional and ethical tradition through the years that now spans three generations. Dan, his father, and his sons are bound by a love of law, order, and their country. Dan's older brother is a colonel in the Army, his half-brother is a major in the Air Force, and his uncle was a Marine.

Dan's father spent most of his career serving the US government as a soldier, working with lepers, and later as a State Department employee. While his father was gathering intelligence to help locate

POWs shot down over the Ho Chi Minh Trail, Dan marveled at the shaking of the ground when B-52's were on patrol and watched the T-28 Loa fighter planes land near his elementary school in Laos, where his father was stationed. Over time, his respect for the pilots grew and he decided he wanted to become a pilot. Unfortunately, his eyesight wasn't good enough so he joined the Army with a hope to join the Explosive Ordinance Disposal (EOD).

In addition to watching planes land, Dan listened to many stories about the brave soldiers who detonated unexploded cluster bombs. As a child, the soldiers he saw and heard about while in Thailand and Laos were to be revered. As a man, becoming a soldier, and later a bomb technician, was a dream come true.

Dan's upbringing in a military family with a strong Christian background set the stage for his future; he set off to make a difference in the world. His journey began at the University of Minnesota where he joined the ROTC, got commissioned as an officer, and met his future wife, Wendy.

A full moon on Friday the 13th is rare, and Dan and Wendy felt they had found a rare love in one another; so, it seemed logical that Dan proposed to Wendy under just such a moon in the airport garage. After flying in from Ft. Bliss, he handed her a ring and said, "Here, try this on, see if it fits." A simple, straightforward proposal, fitting for this couple.

After Dan was commissioned as an Army lieutenant, they married, Dan graduated, went to Germany for active duty as an Air Defense Artillery Officer, and Wendy stayed behind to finish school--

until she found out she was pregnant. One day after Dan arrived in Germany, Wendy called him with the news. It didn't take Wendy long to quit school and move to Germany to be with Dan.

Dan and Wendy spent three years in Germany; they bore a child, watched the Berlin Wall come down, and began what seemed to them to be the perfect life together. During this time, Dan served as a platoon leader and liaison to NATO forces, coordinated trainings and conducted briefings on Air Defense issues for a Mechanized Infantry Brigade and German army units.

Eventually, Dan would transfer to the US Army Reserves where he was promoted to captain in the Psychological Operations Unit. He later transferred to inactive reserve and received an honorable discharge in 2000. As a child, Dan had always wanted to be a bomb technician, and, although he didn't have the opportunity in the military, he set his sights on this new goal again--with the Minneapolis Police Department.

The mid-nineties was an infamous time for Minneapolis, aka Murderapolis. With a surge in violent crime and a murder rate higher than New York City, it was a difficult place to live. Dan loved police work and with the busy schedule he thrived. In the 1990's alone, Dan earned two Department Awards of Merit, a Medal of Commendation and Unit Citation, a Medal of Valor, and attended multiple trainings through the FBI, the military and other law enforcement agencies. He spent time in the gang unit, homicide, and the juvenile unit. Dan's ethnic background also served him well. With a large Southeast

Asian population, Dan helped form a liaison between the community and the police department. He served the city well and faithfully.

As the calendar turned to the year 2000, the murder rate in Minneapolis began to drop. But the world became a more dangerous place after 9-11. Bomb squads evolved, and Dan finally realized his dream of being a full time bomb technician. After attending ATF, anti-terrorism and counter terrorism trainings around the country, Dan, now a sergeant, became the full time bomb squad commander. In 2004, Dan was sent to Israel for even more training.

According to Dan and Wendy's kids, "life was perfect." They had everything a young family could have wanted. Dan had his dream job, Wendy had started a web design business while she served on the city council, their oldest child was on a state championship swim team and their youngest was in second grade. With strong faith, they continued to believe it was more important to do good things than to make lots of money.

Dan loved teaching. Ironically, a training exercise would end his career.

Explosive breaching is a technique used to gain entry into a room or building with the use of explosives, a technique Dan had been taught, used, and taught others. It's a specific science and can be dangerous if not performed correctly. When a bomb detonates, the explosion generates a tremendous amount of pressure which creates blast waves. Additionally, the waves' energy can be reflected back in toward the middle of the blast area, and those waves can combine, like waves in an ocean, to create much more powerful waves in certain areas.

Using explosives is dangerous business, and, to minimize the danger, bomb technicians have a series of instruments and formulas to help calculate safe distances from the bomb and what size stack to use in different breach scenarios. The calculator Dan had only computed the initial pressure because the reflected pressures are impossible to calculate--but the makers of the calculator didn't tell the users that. There are too many variables involved to safely calculate any outcome from a bomb blast, not even with the use of a super computer.

On February 5, 2005, Dan's team continued their training and data collection. Using an old school building slated for demolition, they calculated, blasted, logged their findings, and learned. Dan performed about 15 breaches that day, each with a goal of teaching safety and entry after the blast. Each blast was preceded by a series of calculations using a breaching calculator provided to them by the ATF. In a building with concrete ceilings and floors and cinder block walls, a lot of variables existed. The team carefully entered all of the information. After one particular blast, Dan felt strange; he had a terrible headache and was nauseous. Not seeing it as a warning signal, Dan thought he was simply tired from the long day of training.

That afternoon Dan still didn't quite feel like himself, so he told his co-workers he wasn't feeling well and went home with what he thought was a developing sinus infection. The next morning, his doctor gave him antibiotics and sent him home. As the week wore on, Dan felt worse and his doctor prescribed a different type of antibiotic. By now, Dan's face started to droop and one pupil was larger than the other. Believing he had Bell's palsy, he called his old friend and Army doctor, Major Allen Autrey, who sent Dan back to his doctor armed with information about Horner's syndrome.

Dan's doctor thought it unlikely he had a brain injury and sent him to an eye doctor. The eye doctor immediately sent him to the emergency room where they performed an MRI; they saw nothing unusual but kept him overnight for observation. Unfortunately, medicine isn't an exact science and sometimes things are missed, wrongly diagnosed, or not understood. Dan would experience all of these things on his medical journey.

When a new doctor arrived for his shift in the morning, he noticed Dan's MRI had been misread. Dan's carotid artery was dissecting and blood was not flowing properly. Dan's decision making was off; he was ordering strange combinations of food, chalking it up to exhaustion and his desire to go home. Still not recognizing his brain injury, the hospital sent Dan home with Heparin, a blood thinner.

When he arrived home, he quickly deteriorated. He began to feel worse, light bothered him, and he curled into a ball hoping the pain would subside. Luckily, Dr. Autrey hadn't forgotten his friend; he called to check on Dan. Hearing he was in such bad shape, he made a few phone calls which enabled Dan to be seen at the ER immediately. Despite the fact he felt terrible, Dan didn't know why Dr. Autrey was making such a fuss. He was a cop, and cops get hurt. He had no idea how serious things were about to become.

Dan didn't stay in the ER for long. He was rushed by ambulance to the stroke center. Due to his artery getting worse, the doctors believed a massive fatal stroke was imminent. The more the carotid artery collapsed, the less blood flowed to Dan's brain. Dan jokingly stated, "Bomb technicians don't need a blood flow to their heads, we don't use our brains."

By now, it was clear Dan's life was in grave danger and the doctors believed surgery wasn't an option considering his high risk for a stroke. Luckily for Dan, his other blood vessels were pumping just enough blood to keep him going but not enough to prevent brain damage, allow him to perform much physical exercise, or reduce the emotional injuries he and his family were about to receive.

When Dan was injured in 2005, doctors, scientists, and military personnel were just starting to realize the impact of bomb blasts on the brain. Unfortunately, police departments weren't making the connection between bomb blasts and Traumatic Brain Injury (TBI). Minneapolis was no different.

Because Dan had been so ill, and he had short term memory loss, initially he didn't tell the doctors about the breaching and that the symptoms began to appear immediately afterward. Now a few weeks after the breaching, Wendy called the police department to let them know what was going on and to ask for help from his union. Since Minneapolis administers its own insurance and workers compensation, Wendy provided all of the necessary information and was told they would investigate her claim and get back to her. When she asked how they were to survive without income, she was told, "That is not my problem."

Dan and Wendy survived off of his sick and vacation time until it ran out, and the generosity of other officers who donated their vacation time to Dan got them through another three months. Dan had dedicated his life in service to his country and his community. He and his family sacrificed a lot over the years and didn't ask for anything in return. When he was in need, as a direct result of his service, some from his community turned on him. Treating him as though he were trying to scam the city, they refused to believe he was injured on the job or that they were liable for his injuries. Although required to make rulings on workers compensation claims within fourteen days, Minneapolis took six months before making a decision about Dan.

During those six months, Dan and his family worried about how they would survive financially, how Dan would get treatment, and, more importantly, how to survive intact. Dan's three sons had trouble processing what was happening. The abandonment by the city and the change in their father's personality became too much, so they did what teenagers do: they began acting out. The entire family dynamic changed, and Wendy became the head of the household. She had to discipline the children, take care of the home, and now take care of Dan. Because of his brain injury, Dan could no longer do many things. He needed Wendy's full attention.

While Dan's family tried to cope with the after-effects of his injury and the city decided whether or not they would award benefits, Dr. Autrey tried to figure out what had happened to Dan. In the first months after his injury, he still had no diagnosis other than the collapsed artery. Dr. Autrey believed there was more to what was going on, so he reviewed Dan's medical records and contacted a surgeon at Walter Reed National Medical Military Center to find out about bomb-induced brain injuries. There was a soldier being treated for the same injuries as Dan and Dr. Autrey was finding out everything he could about the symptoms, diagnosis, and treatment.

Meanwhile, Dan's situation became increasingly difficult.

The city had finally approved Dan's workers compensation claim but, since they administered the benefits, they stepped in and began making decisions for his care. The city's workers comp nurse was pressuring his medical providers to decide that Dan's symptoms were psychosomatic. As a result, his neurologist stopped even examining him and berated him to just get over the symptoms. Each step forward became two steps back. The decisions weren't always based on medical facts; they were based on what they *believed* was wrong with him. Minneapolis wanted Dan to be permanently disabled, because it greatly reduced their financial liability, due to loopholes in state law. They didn't, however, want him to be diagnosed with a brain injury, because that would increase some of their medical costs.

Although Dan was desperate to get back to work, he thought he was going crazy and was afraid to tell people what was going on.

Dan's neurologist sent him to a psychiatrist, to deal with his supposed psychosomatic symptoms. The psychologist decided that the symptoms were more likely real, and sent him to a speech pathologist.

Seeing a speech pathologist turned out to be the turning point in Dan's treatment. The doctor immediately recognized Dan had a brain injury and told him he wasn't crazy. Dan teared up at his words; he never told anyone he felt crazy, but the speech pathologist knew people with undiagnosed brain injuries think they are losing their minds.

The city and the department were contributing to Dan's feelings of craziness. Too many people believed his injury was all in Dan's head and he would get better if he would just admit it and move on. The city of Minneapolis simply refused to believe Dan, and they believed Dr. Autrey's assistance was secured as a way to get more money, not to arrive at a diagnosis. Dan was sent to the Courage Center for six months. After 15 months, he finally was able to get brain injury treatment. They saved his life.

"We went to a mediator who said that the city had to allow treatment, and that Dr. Autrey should be consulted, but we needed someone else as the primary, treating physician. By that time, we were beyond exhausted, and agreed to see the rehab specialist, because we didn't know where else to go. Even as Dan was going through the Courage Center and everything there was confirming he had a brain injury, the city refused to acknowledge the brain injury", Wendy said tiredly. "We went several years with just our family physician and a psychologist from Courage Center. When I finally worked up the energy to ask for another neurologist, the city fought it for months. When they finally did start to pay him, he retired, and again we had to find another one. During this same time period, the city refused to pay for his psychologist for more than 2 years. Fortunately, he was willing to treat Dan without getting paid.

"While all of this was going on, the city hired 'independent medical examinations' to bolster their claims Dan was not really injured. There are doctors who make a very good living writing reports for insurance companies, saying people are faking. Unlike regular doctors, who can be sued for malpractice, they face no liability for the medical claims they make in their reports. Each time Dan would go through one of these exams, he would slide backwards in his adjustment to his brain injury because Dr. So-and-So said he didn't really have a brain injury, and didn't need to rest, or whatever."

During Dan's tenure as a Minneapolis Police Officer, he'd been hit in the head with a set of brass knuckles with spikes attached to them. He needed his scalp stapled. While chasing suspects, their Suburban hit an embankment and Dan's cruiser followed suit deploying the airbags; Dan's face looked like it had been used as a punching bag. During another 20 mile pursuit, the suspect tried to run Dan off the road and he came away with a bloodied and bruised arm. He always fought the good fight, but he left each one with emotional and often physical scars.

Some would say the city had a responsibility to Dan and others like him; they were taking risks with their lives and their well-being for the good of the community. People rally around officers who retire after 20 years on the job and they gather round the families of officers who die in the line of duty. But what happens to those that are permanently disabled? Are they honored? Are their medical costs covered? Do they receive their pensions? Not always. Sometimes the next fight they have is not a good fight; it's a dirty fight just to try to save the city money. Disabled officers are sometimes seen as criminals, liars, and quitters.

Wendy was refused meetings with the mayor and the city blocked her efforts to apply for a Justice Department grant which helps the families of officers killed or disabled in the line of duty. In Minnesota, if an injured officer can find other work and his new salary plus his pension is less than 125% of his salary when leaving the department, workers compensation will provide the funds so that they are making 125% of their previous salary. A permanently disabled officer is allowed 60% of his pension and nothing more. (Minnesota, 2015) Wendy testified in front of the Minnesota legislature to increase the disabled police and firefighter's pension from 60 to 75 percent of their salaries, and she watched as legislation was narrowly passed allowing Dan to collect this pension while dismissing every other disabled officer in the state. There was supposed to be a follow up study to look at taking care of all disabled officers, but it never happened. Due to inflation, Dan's pension is now down to about 60% of what he would be making if he was still able to work.

Disability is viewed as a catch-22. There are those that truly deserve it, and there are others who will abuse the system. The people that truly need it face a tremendous uphill battle physically, emotionally, and politically.

Becoming permanently disabled is a nightmare for most police officers; there is nothing left for them. They receive no closure, often no commendations, and they are quickly forgotten. Dan did not receive a ceremony to thank him for his service. No honor from the mayor. Just a letter telling him his benefits had been cut off. A man who gave it all, loved his career, and believed in honor, decency, and respect was tossed aside like yesterday's news. Just another officer medically retired without recognition. His retirement credentials arrived unceremoniously in the mail five years later.

It's not easy to be forgotten. Dan knows many officers injured in the line of duty become suicidal. His friend Duy Ngo became one of those statistics. Duy Ngo was shot by another officer while working undercover, and, seven years later, haunted by too many demons, Duy killed himself. Dan now feels as though he somehow failed Duy, that he could have helped him because Dan is being haunted by those same demons. He is devastated by his injury and his inability to be a police officer and the husband and father he once was. There is no provision for Dan, just as there wasn't for Duy, for mental health care.

Although Dan sees a psychologist, it's a constant battle to get his benefits to pay the bill.

Trying to find the proper care in a civilization where only a small part of the population will ever understand what you are going through is a burden many first responders are saddled with. PTSI, injuries, and politics weigh heavily on the officer, yet we continue to turn a blind eye to them. We have made officers into robotic super heroes that aren't allowed feelings, intellect, or human error. They have been ostracized by society and stripped of their basic human behaviors.

We also have yet to admit there are husbands, wives, children, and parents actively involved in these officers' lives hoping to help them cope with their trauma. Families who do more than make sure they get enough sleep, a hot meal and fresh uniforms in the closet. The faces of the families are yet to be seen.

Before Dan's injury, he was very active; he loved to mountain bike, snowboard, and play baseball. Since he would no longer enjoy these sports, he found a way to honor injured soldiers and officers by forming a snowmobile racing team named "Sheer Determination." Dan can't race, he needs adult supervision most of the time so he doesn't set the garage on fire (again), and his critical thinking skills aren't what they used to be. Dan is learning to improvise, adapt, and overcome to stop doing things before they cause him harm. Dan describes his injury as a muddy embankment: he keeps trying to climb up but the mud makes him slide down toward the river each time he starts to make his way forward.

Despite this, he volunteers his time speaking to injured officers and trying to make people understand
the dangers of breaching. Wendy helped found a
non-profit organization dedicated to helping injured
police officers.

Wendy also suffers from depression; she's had
panic attacks and gained weight. Adrenaline kept
her going for a long time--things needed to be done,
so she did them. She didn't recognize she was in
shock and she was barely getting through the day.

Coping with her feelings became a battle. The
hardest part for Wendy was the hostility from the
city.

"I can deal with it when Dan is uncooperative,
because I know he doesn't mean what he is saying,
and does care about me. It hurts, a lot, but I can usually let it go. But when I ask for help from the city,
they are so cruel. We asked for respite care, and they
spent a year and a half fighting us in court. It was
completely absurd, but the judge agreed with them.
A lot of times, it felt like Alice in Wonderland. If they
were telling the truth, I would be ok with it, but
when they lie about us to keep us from having any
help, it makes things so hard. There is no hope when
you have to fight against lies.

"The city has minimized their support for us because they believed the federal government would
step in. Some people have even testified that we
shouldn't get any state benefits because of the federal benefits – which we haven't received yet. People
on the city level aren't allowed to help us pursue federal benefits because it might conflict with their

quest to avoid liability. It's very difficult to for us to fight a political machine."

Despite the battles, Dan didn't want Wendy to be angry at Minneapolis because it made him feel like he wasted his life on something worthless. Eventually they agreed they could be mad at the people who were mistreating them, but not with all of the people in Minneapolis because that would mean he risked most of his adult life for nothing.

Wendy also had to mourn the loss of "old Dan" and learn to love the "new Dan." She still misses old Dan sometimes, but tries not to think about it too much. In 2013, she successfully battled cancer, and it was scary to think that Dan would never be able to take care of her. She's not sure what's going to happen when they get old. She tries not to think too much about the future, either.

Their children have recovered and forgiven the profession they had become so disenchanted with after Dan's injury. They were young, hurt, and didn't know how to cope. They didn't know what to do when they saw their invincible father so broken and helpless. The man that was supposed to lead them through life now naps, has a difficult time in crowds, and can't even go to the mall with them. When the oldest son graduated from high school, Dan fell over multiple times during the ceremony. His brain now sees things differently and his equilibrium is off. Wendy spent six months working with the school to accommodate Dan's handicap so that he could attend the graduation of his youngest son this year.

Dan's older children call him regularly to check in; they've apologized for their behavior immediately following the injury and have accepted it. His oldest son joined the Army and did a tour in Afghanistan. His middle son is now a bomb technician in the Army and his youngest son just started college.

They've lost a lot of friends and gained some new ones in the form of other injured officers. Dan and Wendy have accepted that injuries not only change your life, but also the way people see you. We often have a more difficult time adjusting to other families' problems than we do to our own.

Dan and Wendy are also aware of the statistics: Dan is fifty times more likely than the rest of us to commit suicide, and the divorce rate for couples with a brain-injured spouse is high. They believe God and stubbornness will get them through. "There's more to life than money. We don't have any regrets and we will continue to raise awareness." They firmly believe there is something more. That when you are doing something for a just cause and the freedom of others there is honor and dignity.

Dan feels broken, but not worthless. "In the eyes of man I may have worn out my usefulness but I don't care what man thinks. Maybe my brain injury is God's answer to something."

MARIO

Some people are lucky enough to find their passion and spend their life pursuing it. Whether it is photography, accounting, sports, or law enforcement, they immerse themselves in the occupation that suits them. They refine their craft and look forward to a lifetime of going to the office knowing they love what they do and there are no regrets. When a life is irreversibly altered in a way that prohibits a person from continuing along their beloved path, they may feel depressed, angry, or like the shell of the person they once were. When the life is intentionally altered by someone else, the person can be left in a purgatory of sorts, hoping in a child-like fashion that things may somehow reverse themselves and they can return to the profession they loved so much. Mario is the epitome of a man whose dream was stolen, and he hasn't quite found a way to accept or believe it.

His journey to becoming a police officer was unremarkable; he didn't come from a law enforcement family but came from a family of six boys whose father worked in a factory. Mario always wanted to help people, nothing more; he believed law enforcement would give him that opportunity.

While waiting for a position on the police department to open up, Mario worked as a dispatcher which made his transition to the streets relatively easy. He knew the streets and the officers he would be working with. He worked nights on patrol for seven years before becoming a detective, and in 2009 he was assigned to the Federal Bureau of Alcohol,

Tobacco, Firearms and Explosives (ATF) where he thrived while working undercover operations and gun buys. He speaks with pride when he tells you that he and his brother were the first brothers to become detectives in Somerville and the first brothers to serve on a federal task force at the same time. His brother served on the bank robbery task force, Mario with the ATF.

Mario loved his job, and he was fair but firm. "It's easier to cultivate trust and informants if you find balance; you can't be a pushover or a hard ass all the time. A good cop has the right balance; he knows when to tone it down and when to be a tough guy."

Although he worked the busiest area of the city, he found there was a softer side of policing. He was able to find and connect with groups of people he may not have otherwise; the city was open to him in a way he never imagined. He particularly enjoyed his work with the elderly. He always made time for them and ensured that the elderly center on his route had shrubs and landscaping donated whenever they needed it.

Mario also connected with the city in many life-saving ways, some of which almost cost him his own life. One such incident came about all because a woman couldn't speak English. She called 9-1-1 and rather than report a fire, she reported a fight. Because the fire trucks hadn't been dispatched, Mario was first on the scene and the first to hear the cries for help emanating from the burning house. Without hesitation, or proper gear, he entered the house three times to remove people from the home. Admittance to the hospital for smoke inhalation was a small price to pay for saving lives. His own safety was merely an afterthought.

Somerville was busy, and Mario liked it that way. During his first year with the ATF, undercover assignments took him out of state and he helped take over 200 guns off the streets. Despite his proximity to guns, and the dangerous people who carried them, he had never been involved in a shooting.

By 2010, Mario was one of the most decorated officers on the Somerville Police Department with more than twenty awards, including the Somerville Police Officer of the Year three times, Somerville Police Detective of the Year twice, three Medals of Valor, two Life Saving Awards, and the ATF Director's Award.

At home, Mario was just as successful. He had a loving wife and a son he adored. Mario and Christy married on November 5, 2005 and she never questioned his chosen profession or his loyalty to it. "I have the best wife; she is so understanding. I think that's one reason I have been able to maintain a decent state of mind. Details, undercover work, she always understood."

Mario's son Drew and a man named Matthew Krister entered Mario's life in the same year. While Drew would bring joy to Mario's life, Krister would bring devastation.

In December 2007, Krister arranged a meeting in Somerville with some kids looking to sell stolen stereo equipment. Rather than purchase the equipment as arranged, Krister robbed them at gunpoint. When two criminals are involved in a crime, things typically don't end well. Luckily, this day would pass without incident. The stereo thieves returned home empty-handed; they didn't press charges because they had stolen the equipment. When police found the gun used in the robbery three weeks later, they couldn't connect it to Krister. He flew under the radar until October 2010.

As part of the ATF task force, Mario's job was to follow-up on any alerts raising concern about gun purchases. When someone buys a lot of guns in a short amount of time, the dealer is required to send an alert to the ATF. The ATF then investigates the involved parties, and, depending on the quantity and type of guns and the purchaser's background, this can include a trip to the purchaser's home to see if there is any reason for concern.

From October 8 to October 18, 2010, Krister purchased ten handguns in New Hampshire (NH). The case fell on Mario's lap because Krister still lived in Somerville, Massachusetts. Mario didn't recognize the name immediately, although it seemed familiar; the minute he opened the old case file he recalled the previous incident and realized it was worth further investigation. He thought, "Oh shit, now this kid is buying guns?"

It didn't take long to find Krister was up to something. He had obtained a New Hampshire address even though he was living in Somerville, and they would later find out Krister paid someone to put his name on a lease so he could prove residency and obtain a NH driver's license. He purchased his first gun a mere two hours after receiving his NH driver's license.

"He has a driver's license in two different states which is illegal; I knew something was afoot. With his background, he should not be buying guns. Luckily, he had just been stabbed and it gave us a reason to talk to him without raising suspicion."

At the time Mario had a new ATF agent with him, and he had just finished field training and was a go-getter. Mario liked working cases with him because they both took pride in taking guns off the street. In less than a month, this agent would drag Mario's bullet-ridden body to safety.

Getting Krister to the police station was the last easy thing that would happen with this case. His cell phone number was on file from the recent stabbing; Krister had a minor wound in his shoulder from an altercation at a party. The police told Krister they had a suspect in the stabbing and he was needed to look at a photo array. He happily arrived at the station the next night to identify the suspect.

Mario and his partner waited outside so they could record Krister's car make, model and plate number. Krister, suspicious, parked two blocks away and walked to the station negating any chance to find out what he was driving.

When Krister was seated, Mario asked to see his driver's license. Krister handed him his NH license.

"Don't you live in Somerville with your mother?"

"Yes, here's my Massachusetts license."

"It's illegal to have a driver's license in more than one state. We know you obtained one in NH to buy guns. You're not here for a photo array. We want to talk to you about the guns."

Krister turned white and stammered about the guns, all ten of them, being stolen during a break-in at his fictitious NH residence. It wasn't long before Krister confessed to buying the guns for $350 each, using a Dremel to file off the serial numbers, and selling them to gang members for $1,500 each. Krister provided Mario and his partner with the names of some very dangerous gang members. Krister also admitted to parking his car two blocks away because he had two guns in the trunk.

"You're 21-years-old. Do the right thing. We want the gang; we want the people that are on the street killing others with these guns. Make a deal with us and we'll help you," Mario said. "We'll give you some guns that have no firing pins; you make a call and set up a meeting with the buyers."

Krister called the buyer. Using street lingo he set up a meeting for the next day promising to bring puppies (guns) and dog food (ammo).

Krister was scared. These people were dangerous and he knew if they found out he was working with the cops he'd be dead. Mario discussed witness protection with him and instinctively hugged him.

"We'll get you through this. I'll see you here in the morning and we will get through this together. There are ten guns on the street and we need to right the wrong before innocent people get killed."

As an investigator, it's important to be aware of what the other guy is doing, and Mario had created social media accounts posing as a woman so he could friend people that were important to his investigations and the community. He wanted to know what they were doing at all times. Krister left the station, got home and wrote, "Fuck the Somerville police and fuck the ATF, I'm gonna do me and do me strong," on his Facebook page. Mario printed a copy and put it in the file.

The next morning Mario arrived at the station, prepared the paperwork, got the gun ready for sale and waited for Krister. He didn't show up. They tried Krister's cell phone. No answer. They drove by his house multiple times but saw no car.

That night, Krister called Mario from a blocked number.

"Matt, we can't help you if you aren't on board. Help us get these guns off the street."

"Fuck you, I'm not helping you." And he hung up.

Warrants were issued for Krister's arrest for trafficking firearms over state lines. Mario and his partner drove by Krister's house a few more times, but he was gone; they couldn't serve the warrants and arrest him. With Krister never far from their minds, it was back to business as usual for Mario and his partner.

On Nov 2, 2010 the sun rose as it did any other day, Mario said goodbye to his wife and son, and headed to work. He and his partner planned to work the night shift; they had an informant willing to work with the Feds but had requested to work with Mario. Mario planned to work a detail, sign up the new informant, call it an early night, maybe get a few beers, and then go home.

Mario went to his detail, worked out at the gym, showered, changed into jeans and a sweatshirt and went to the station. The new informant called to let Mario know he was working late and would come to the station at 8pm instead of 6pm.

"We haven't been by Krister's house in over a week, let's take a ride by and back up the guys on the street while we're waiting."

Mario and his partner headed out with only their guns and their radios. No cuffs, no vests, no extra equipment. They weren't planning to do anything but help out where needed. Not wearing a vest wasn't unusual for Mario. It was too easy to spot when you were working undercover. They were simply killing time before they had to meet with the informant.

As they turned down Krister's street, Mario's partner said, "What if the kid's car is here?"

"You spoke too soon. There it is," replied Mario. Krister's red two-door Honda coupe was parked in front of his mother's house.

It was 5:30pm on election night, and the streets, although dark, were busy. People were voting, driving home from work or heading out to dinner. Mario parked across the street from Krister's house behind a function hall and called his sergeant; they had a federal warrant for Krister's arrest and they wanted to execute it as seamlessly as possible.

Plainclothes officers quickly arrived on scene along with the sergeant in patrol and the sergeant of detectives. They potentially had a man who had been on the run with access to guns in the house across the street. They didn't know if he had loaned his car to someone or if he was inside the house. Complicating matters, his mother arrived home.

They knew they didn't have much time to make a decision. It could be over an hour before the SWAT team was able to gear up and arrive. They also knew they had used up their opportunity to bluff him when they brought him in for questioning a few weeks prior.

Then the decision was made for them: the porch light turned on, Krister exited onto the deck, turned and waved to his mother before descending the stairs.

Mario and his team had seconds to act. They knew they could not let him get into his car. There were too many pedestrians and other drivers to risk any kind of chase or erratic driving. They needed to get to him before he could drive off. They quickly decided Mario's partner would position his car in front of Krister's and another officer would block the rear of the vehicle preventing him from going anywhere. Mario was the closest on foot.

Krister got to his car and opened the door.

Mario called over the radio, "Move in! Move in!"

As the police vehicles blocked Krister's car, Mario's partner hit his front end. Krister, stunned, allowed Mario time to open the car door and place him at gunpoint.

"Get out of the car, Matt."

"Shoot me! Fucking shoot me!"

Mario thought, "What's wrong with this kid? He wants me to kill him."

In a fraction of a minute, the unthinkable happened. Krister straightened his legs against the floorboard of the car making it difficult for Mario to pull him out. While thinking, "If my gun goes off and I kill him, I am out of a job. I will lose my career and kill someone unarmed," another officer ran up on the car in Mario's peripheral vision. He never saw the gun. Flicking his eyes up quickly, he only looked back when he saw the flashes. Krister's gun had been in his right hand out of Mario's sight.

Krister shot Mario six times at point blank range.

Pop. Into the right side of his chest, missing the heart by two millimeters and going through the liver. *Pop.* Another to the chest. *Pop.* To the stomach, through the colon, the hip bone and lodged into the lower back. *Pop.* To the stomach. *Pop.* To the stomach. *Pop.* Through the forearm and out the elbow.

"I saw flashes and heard pops. I remember shaking, like getting punched like a punching bag. I fell back and yelled, 'I've been hit.'"

Mario's partner was next to Mario when he was shot. When the shooting started, he retreated to the back of the car and returned fire. The sergeant who was running up to the car shot into the passenger window, and the officer in front of the car also began shooting. The three officers never saw each other. They had tunnel vision. All they saw was Mario get hit and their goal was to take out the threat.

Lying on the street, still conscious, Mario heard the gunfire of the other officers. Confused and trying to make sense of what had happened, he watched his partner run up, grab his shirt and drag him behind a car leaving him there. His partner had lost a buddy in Iraq when their Humvee blew up, and he wasn't going to lose Mario; he wanted to get Mario out of the range of more gunshots. He went back to his position behind the car.

Krister shot first; there was no time to tell him to put the gun down. Mario could hear the gunfire, the mother screaming, "My son, my son, that's my son!" He heard another officer, "Get back in the house!" *Pop. Pop. Pop.* But the loudest voice he could hear was his own.

"Now things are starting to sink in. I reach up and feel my chest. I tried to sit up and shoot him but I realize I got shot in the arm; I couldn't lift the arm or sit up. I could feel the blood oozing out of me and remember feeling thick red blood everywhere. I thought, 'Oh my God, I got shot in the chest!' I started to panic and thought, 'Fuck. I am not going home tonight, this is it. This is it. I am going to die next to a parked car. I'll never see my family again, my son, my wife, my parents, nobody.' I wondered what would happen as I died. Was an angel going to appear? Am I going to look down on this scene and see my body lying in the street?

"You can practice all you like; there are no rules out on the street. No one is going to stand where the instructor tells them; you can't stop and look at your position. You'll be dead. If you've never been in a shooting, don't decide what should have been done. It's do or die. You won't see or hear anything but the beating of your own heart and the prayer you are saying to make it home."

In the background Mario could hear, "Crossfire! Crossfire! Watch your crossfire!" The officers couldn't see or hear each other over the sixty rounds being fired. They are lucky they didn't hit each other.

Mario knew he had to try to save himself until help arrived. So he breathed. He remembered, as many properly trained officers do, that he could minimize his blood loss if he controlled his breathing.

"Put me in the cruiser! Get me out of here! I'm losing too much blood!"

The gunfire had stopped and he was now being attended by his friends. They were ripping off his clothes yelling, "Hole! Hole!"

"How many holes do I have?"

"The ambulance will be here any minute."

"No! Take me to the hospital now! I won't make it!"

"Don't move him! Hold pressure! He's aspirating!"

Mario's eyes rolled back in his head.

One of his friends broke down; falling to the ground weeping, he called his parents.

"Mom, there's been a shooting. It's not me. I am going to watch Mario die." And he wept.

Another officer took his gun away, and another told him to get his act together before the camera crews arrived. There was no time to grieve; no time to call loved ones, no time to process the trauma. Just move forward and put on a brave face.

"Is he gonna make it?!"

The paramedic said, "I don't think he's gonna make the trip."

"Fuck you I'm not," Mario answered.

Mario received IVs and pressure where pressure was needed.

"Stay with me, Mario."

"You better save me; I need to get home to my little boy. Do your job. I need to get home. I'll do mine."

"You have two little boys?"

"What are you fucking stupid? I said I have one little boy."

The Massachusetts State Police provided a six car escort trying to get the ambulance to the hospital in time.

At the ER, an older nurse with dark hair and thick glasses looked right into his face, held his left arm and said, "You're gonna be okay; you're gonna be alright." She kept repeating it over and over, so close Mario could smell her breath. The lights were bright as Mario was rushed into the operating room. "The same nurse kept getting in my face telling me I was going to be okay. I said, 'just put me to sleep.' I was so tired of fighting. I just wanted to sleep. It was so hard to fight."

While Mario was lying on the street bleeding, his wife Christy pulled into her driveway and wondered what Mario was up to. She changed her clothes, took off her make-up and put their son Drew in the tub thinking that the day was finally over and she could relax.

Suddenly, she heard the doorbell ringing. Not just ringing, someone was leaning on it. Then the phone began to ring.

She got Drew out of the tub, answered the phone and began walking down the stairs. Her mother-in-law was on the other end of the phone crying. As Christy opened the front door and saw two police officers standing there, she heard them say, "Mario has been shot," at the same time her mother in law said, "Did anyone call you? Mario's been hurt."

"There are two police officers at the door. I will call you back."

Christy backed away from the door and the officers entered her house. The officers weren't in uniform, or even in a cruiser; they were a married law enforcement couple that lived a few streets over and they had brought their son with them to deliver the news. With no formal notification process in place, they were the quickest way to reach Christy and bring her to the hospital.

They told her Mario was at Mass General and he was going into surgery. "I held onto that thought, that he wasn't dead. He was shot. That is what made me hold it together," Christy said. "I don't know if I would have felt any different if he was dead; I think I would have lost my mind. But I had hope; I thought, 'some really good doctors were working on him.' That gave me hope."

"I have to get Drew dressed, I need to pack a bag and I can follow you."

"No, you are not following us. Go upstairs and get your stuff. We need to go."

"I remember walking upstairs like it was slow motion. Trying so hard to keep it together. Because if I started crying I would have to explain why to Drew. I couldn't do that. I told him we were going for a ride. We'll get some toys and go for a ride. He didn't pick up on my sadness, which was good. We got our stuff. I locked up the house and got in the neighbor's truck."

Christy found herself in the front seat of an off-duty cop's vehicle speeding down the highway with a 3-year-old in her lap. She couldn't call anyone to tell them what happened because she had Drew with her and she didn't want him to know, didn't want him to hear her cry. From her phone, she e-mailed her boss to let them know she wouldn't be at work the next day but she still wasn't sure why. The vague notification scared her more than she wanted to admit.

"The rest is a blur; I got to the hospital and was met by a staff member who brought me to the tiniest closed-in room. Mario's parents and some of his brothers were already there with some close family friends. No one really knew what to say to each other. I just kept thinking, 'I'm not gonna cry; I'm gonna have hope and pray.' I took it upon myself to be the strong one. I needed to be strong for Drew; I didn't want him to see me cry."

After losing Mario three times, the doctors arrived to tell Christy he had pulled through, was in recovery, and was going to be okay.

"I just remember being so thankful. Thank God my husband was going to be okay. I thanked the doctor; I appreciated what he had done. There weren't words for it. He just saved my husband's life and I'd never forget that. Anything could have happened. He could have handed it off to someone else, it could have been a different night with a less experienced doctor, but it wasn't. He saved Mario's life."

Mario woke two days later and met Dr. David King, a man who had served as a lieutenant colonel in the army and had learned to handle major trauma after serving two tours overseas; he would later go on to save some of the Boston Marathon bombing victims.

"I got shot six times? Where is the nurse that held my hand? I want to thank her." Mario described the nurse to his doctor.

"We don't have a nurse like that here Mario; the trauma team met you at the door. There was no nurse."

Mario remembers her vividly, whoever she was. She held his hand and kept Mario with them.

Mario described his release, "I got a nice escort home. The only problem was that my sutures ruptured and I was bleeding all over the house. We had to turn around and go back. Blood all over the house, my poor son was in shock. But they sewed me up and I was still able to go home that night."

A nurse was sent to care for Mario twice a day, and one day she sent Christy to the store to get bigger gauze pads. Christy also picked up a pregnancy test.

"Before the shooting, we were planning to try for another baby in January. I should have had a period but it never came, and I thought it was just stress. I had no symptoms at all, hadn't been eating well and was drinking wine as I always had. When I saw the positive symbol, I almost fell over. I couldn't believe the baby had made it through all that. I knew that since the baby was still there, it was going to be strong."

Within five months, Mario was back to work. He wanted his life back, to be himself again. He wanted to be on the phone making gun deals. He felt like a half-human without his beloved job.

"He wanted to go back to work after being shot; I was behind him 100%, I'm his wife, and I will support him in whatever he wants to do," Christy said. "He's got a strong personality, but he's a good decision maker; he's good at what he does. I trust his judgement. He wanted to go back to work and I supported it. He wanted to feel complete, feel normal. I told him to heal and when he was healed swing back in; and that's what he did. He was a little skittish but it wasn't as apparent to me but I am sure to other people it was because they were by his side."

Eleven months back on the job and Mario had a massive heart attack. He survived, again.

After the heart attack, he convinced himself he could do desk duty when he was better. He would wait longer this time and go back when his body told him to. He waited a year. His body told him he couldn't go back.

"When he had the heart attack, I knew he couldn't go back because of his health. It wasn't an option. He had a major heart attack; he is lucky he survived and that he didn't do more damage to himself," Christy said. "I can't help but wonder, 'How is he so strong mentally and physically?'

"I'm a faithful and religious person. I totally believe 100% that the man upstairs had something to do with this. I told Mario, 'You were kept here for a reason; your work isn't done yet. You can't teach and preach about things unless you've experienced them for yourself. Take this as a sign; it's time to teach and preach.'"

Mario and Christy have a lot to teach and preach about; too many departments aren't prepared for a critical incident like Mario's.

"Delivery of the news and the silent car ride was poor. Everything was handled poorly. It's like no one knew what to do. It was disorganized. Not that I complained, but I didn't know how I was supposed to be told or why it mattered," said Christy. "The news is still going to be the same no matter how they tell me. I don't know how the delivery could have been done differently and I don't want to blame anyone or make them feel badly. They did the best they could do in the chaos."

Mario has teamed up with other violently injured police officers in Massachusetts to form just that: the Violently Injured Police Officers, a peer support group for police officers that have sustained serious permanent injuries during violent encounters in the line of duty. They've helped enact legislation to get officers 100% of their benefits for their lifetimes after a permanent or serious traumatic injury. They now speak to officers around the state about their experiences, how to be prepared, and how to prepare their spouses. Most departments make mistakes. They don't know how to help their officers, they have no notification policies in place, and they don't know officers are now worried about how they are going to feed their kids. The mistakes they make in the time immediately after an incident affect the families for the rest of their lives. Mario wants to help minimize those mistakes.

Despite the positive steps Mario is taking to help other officers, and the fact he has a mission, his first love was, and remains, active policing. He misses his job; he's coped by convincing himself he's still on leave, that he's going back someday. He's conned himself into believing it because that's what he needs to be able to mentally and emotionally cope.

Sometimes Mario feels like an outcast, like he has a disease no one wants to catch. He's not one of the guys anymore; he's not on the streets and in the middle of the action. The fundraisers are over, he's home, and everything has died down.

"I'd give all my medals back to have my job. I miss it so much. It's the only way I can quell the pain," he said. "I have all my credentials, everything, and I don't want to part with it. I don't have a retired badge. I want my boys to see me in uniform again. It sucks so badly. It's my way of coping and minimizing the big letdown. I know it's a pipedream. I slowly try to convince myself of that."

As for Christy, she still loves her husband with all of her heart and supports him as best she can. She knows his experience was different than hers, so every day she tries to do something she knows will help him or make his day easier, whether it's making dinner, having his favorite shirt clean for the weekend, taking the kids out so he can have some time to himself, or changing her schedule so she can spend more time with her family.

"I don't want people to pity us; we are going to move on. Thank God he can walk, talk and use his arms.

"I feel like him being shot transformed him a lot. Now he is able to teach and talk about it. He's become involved with Concerns for Police Survivors; they needed him as much as he needed them. He is now able to tell his story."

In Christy's eyes, police are heroes no matter what; they are there to save and help people.

"It is God that gives them the courage to do their jobs."

She knows not everyone can look at the things he sees and get over them the way Mario does or has. She's a panicker; Mario senses that and helps her calm down. He put things in perspective, and not everyone can do that.

Christy believes, good or bad, that everything happens for a reason. Nearly five years later, neither she nor Mario can talk about the incident without becoming wrought with emotion, but she still believes there was a reason for it.

"I told him, 'This is why you are still here, with us. If you weren't here I would have a little baby boy due around the time of your birthday and I would have named him Mario.'"

After he returned to work, his second son, Tyler David was born. Tyler's middle name was given to him in honor of the man that saved Mario's life, Dr. David King. Dr. King is still a good friend to Mario as is the paramedic that worked on him, the same paramedic that thought Mario had two sons.

Mario is still here, and he witnessed the birth of his second son. On July 30, after only a few hours of labor, Tyler was born. An hour later Christy nursed him, and, when she was done, the nurse subtly took him from Christy and started rubbing him. He had turned purple and Christy didn't even notice. Once he got his color back, the nurse kept her eye on him. The next time, Christy found a lifeless child in her arms. Tyler had stopped breathing.

Tyler spent the following weeks in the NICU of Tufts Hospital in Boston where he continued to have seizures — eighteen seizures in 24 hours. After several invasive tests, they found he had a hemorrhage in his brain and he was put on anti-seizure medication and was kept in the NICU until he was seizure free for an entire week. The first year of Tyler's life wasn't easy with the seizures or medication. But, as his mother predicted, he was strong, as strong as his father. Just before he turned two, Tyler was weaned off the medication and is now seizure free.

Christy can only say to Mario, "This is why God saved your life; I wouldn't have been able to get through this without you."

Mario is now the one that needs help getting through things. On June 30, 2015, he suffered a massive stroke as a direct result of the injuries he incurred the day of his shooting. With two bullets still lodged in his body, it's no surprise. Christy is angry and worried. Mario is depressed and will need more time to process recent events.

With tears in his voice, he called to say that he's mentally drained; some days he wants to give up because he is sick and tired of fighting. "The old me died that night, I'm not the same person. I'm not the same husband, father or man." Since the stroke, his vision has become blurred and he gets confused. Although he was initially paralyzed on his left side, he's gained most of that movement back. Most days, the emotional challenge is greater than the physical.

"When I got shot, my job wasn't just taken away. I felt like a criminal. The only connection I had to my career was my e-mail, which was gone over night. I was left feeling like I did something wrong. I had no badge, no gun and no connection to the department I had loved for so long. I don't think they realize what they do to us when they cut us off. It's hard to live with these injuries knowing that the reason we became injured is no longer part of our lives. We give everything we have to the job and when we are injured, we feel like we no longer exist. That needs to stop. We need better than that; we need to keep our dignity and our sense of accomplishment."

Part Five

COLLATERAL DAMAGE

There are risks and costs to action. But they are far less than the long range risks of comfortable inaction.
                                        - John F. Kennedy

During a traumatic event the focus is usually on the officer directly involved. Unfortunately, the collateral damage that occurs can be far more reaching. Similar to a pebble dropped into a pond, the ripple effects of a traumatic incident such as a line of duty death reach far and wide. Those affected initially will be the other officers on the scene, responding medical personnel, or dispatchers who are coordinating everything over the radio and phone. The family and friends of the officer as they receive notification of the critical incident will be the next to feel the critical incident strain. Finally, the harm will likely continue to echo throughout the entire agency and touch each member. Each person plays their own role in the incident, but the likelihood of a traumatic stress injury is high and needs to be addressed early on if we hope to prevent long-term damage. Agencies should be capable of providing initial trauma support for all involved parties, whether or not the request is made for such services (Blum, 2001). First responders and their family members should have training prior to a critical incident as to what they could expect from themselves and anyone else dealing with psychological trauma. The anxiety of not knowing what is going on with the mind or the body creates a perpetual cycle of ups and downs. Knowledge will help individuals cope with this event and will help them assist others (Artwohl, 2002). Family members need to be trained in how to provide support to a traumatized law enforcement officer, and understand things will never be the same for the officer. LEO children have been found to be susceptible to traumatic stress vicariously through their parents. While things will improve over time, the entire family must find a new routine in order for them to continue to function. Finally, the police family and the real family may find that their needs are different. What would likely be a very private matter with the death or injury of a loved one becomes a community issue when the deceased or injured is a law enforcement officer. Finding a balance is critical for the well-being of the family, the agency, and the community. With all the factual information currently available, law enforcement agencies have a moral obligation to train officers and their families in traumatic stress injuries ahead of time in an effort to soften the blow.

STEPHANIE

Every law enforcement family knows the words they speak before their officer's shift begins could be their last together. Most families see their goodbyes as a ritual and say the same thing each night. For fear of calling attention to the possibility of an on the job injury or death, others treat it as just another departure. Stephanie always said, "I love you. Be safe." Jason always responded, "Always." On June 14, 2013, Jason didn't say, "Always." He said, "I'll try."

Always. Stephanie believed she and Jason would always be together. There was nothing to "try." Their life together was everything she wanted since they met. While working together at the Dillard's department store in Hot Springs, Arkansas, Jason tried to impress Stephanie. Initially, he would wander over from the shoe department, where he worked, to make small talk with Stephanie in the children's department. Although Stephanie felt an immediate attraction to Jason, he needed some prodding to ask Stephanie on a date.

One day while snacking on Skittles, Jason offered some to Stephanie. "I'm diabetic and shouldn't be eating these. Want some?"

"No thanks. I am trying to fit in to a bridesmaid dress that is already too small."

Jason acted indignant. "I can't believe you turned me down," he said, and walked away.

Having witnessed their flirting for a few weeks, a co-worker approached Jason and told him he should stop beating around the bush and ask her out. It was obvious to everyone around them they were head over heels for each other, even if they didn't realize it yet. They married a year later. Skittles were on every table at the reception and a joke between them on each anniversary.

After the wedding, they moved to Sheridan, Arkansas where Jason worked as an EMT. While working on the SWAT team in his capacity as an EMT, Jason began to love police work. He was a thrill seeker and saw the police department could offer him the same adrenaline rush he had come to love as an EMT, but with better hours. Less than a year after they were married, Jason attended the academy and became a member of the Pine Bluff Police Department.

Six years, one child, and two successful careers later, Jason would transfer to the Texarkana Police Department in Texas. Jason was a natural police officer; he took his duties to heart and was happy he had found a profession he loved. Stephanie's kind demeanor and easy smile made her the perfect school teacher. They settled into their new jobs and a new community with less crime and poverty, believing they would always have each other, always have the love and comfort they cherished so much, and that their son would grow up cushioned in that love.

For a law enforcement family, small words can cause great worry. To a LEO spouse, "Can't talk. Busy," or "Be home late, just got called out," can mean anything from a simple car accident to an active shooter. Eventually, the LEO family reminds themselves they can only do their best; they must be patient and not distract their officer with words of worry or concern. More often than not, their officer is safe. But there is always that small voice that says, "Maybe this time they're not. Maybe this time, tragedy will sneak up the walkway of my home in the middle of the night and tell me it's time to come to the hospital."

"Pushing away the 'what if' thoughts are a means of survival, both physically and emotionally. In order to survive as an officer or a family member, we quickly learn to evade and carry on," Stephanie said. "Yet, the stark reality is we are a member of a group that is willing to put their lives on the line for the greater good of the community. The danger is always present, but we tend to believe that ignoring the possibilities is best."

One month shy of their 7 year wedding anniversary, Jason would utter the words that would raise a red flag and make Stephanie want to ask Jason why he would say, "I'll try," instead of, "Always." Although she chose not to point out her anger over what seemed like innocent words, she wondered if he said them accidentally or if he had a premonition the evening would be more difficult than usual.

The evening didn't seem any different than any other. As Jason headed off to his 7pm-7am shift, Stephanie and their son kissed him goodbye and headed off to get her phone fixed. Because it was a weekend, she knew she'd have no contact with Jason if she couldn't text him. Friday and Saturday nights are always the busiest for the night shift.

As it was the first week of summer, Stephanie and her son stayed up late and watched movies. She went to bed at 11pm. Not having heard from Jason after telling him her phone was fixed, she assumed she'd hear from him when he had some free time. She didn't realize the ringer on her phone was turned low.

Meanwhile, Jason was not on patrol on his usual route. A weekend disturbance at Grady T. Wallace Park wasn't unusual. By day, children played soccer and ran through the playground; on weekends, teens and adults gathered for large, often illegal, parties. At midnight on June 14, 2013, Officer Jason Sprague was dispatched to the park in response to reports of more than 100 people gathered with alcohol and drugs. It was a routine call for this area on a summer night.

Jason was the first on the scene, and while there was a long line of cars trying to get out of the park there was no apparent danger; he got out of his patrol vehicle to direct traffic. The party was against city ordinance, but it was often easier to send people on their way rather than cite them if there was no trouble. Jason planned to disburse the crowd just as many other officers were doing in parks around the country that night.

What happened next would show how quickly a simple line of traffic could turn deadly. It would show, whether by accident or intention, how quickly a decision made in haste could change the lives of so many people.

Flashlight in hand, Jason moved the traffic out of the park at a safe pace, a pace which was not acceptable to 21-year-old Justin Sanders. Endangering others, Sanders was driving at a high rate of speed against the flow of traffic. Jason was seen waving his flashlight and making verbal attempts to get the car to stop. At no time did Jason seem distressed or in fear of his life; he was simply waving to the vehicle and repeating the word, "Stop," in an authoritative tone. Proof of this can be heard from the audio of his body microphone. Jason's dash cam records the SUV traveling toward him at a high rate of speed.

With his flashlight in the air, Jason appears about to give another verbal command when Sanders attempts to drive around Jason by driving onto the median. It is this slight turn of the wheel that will cause the SUV to knock Jason to the ground and run over his body.

The SUV which hit Jason stopped briefly; the driver opened his door, looked back and then sped off. A different SUV, traveling in the opposite direction, stopped and an occupant got out of the passenger side and ran to Jason's body. The young man's hand flew to his mouth in surprise, then he quickly ran back to his vehicle and drove away. No one offered Jason any assistance. While shocking to many, it's considered the norm to others.

Jason was left alone on the ground with the flashing of his patrol car's blue lights his only comfort. They flashed over him as if alerting the world that another symbol of order in chaos needed to be guided home.

At 12:40am, Stephanie awoke to pounding on her door. Disoriented, she glanced at her phone. 22 missed calls. Knowing right away something was wrong, she ran to the door, flung it open and said, "Tell me, is he alive?"

"I realized I had spent years trusting that the tried and true evasion tactics would work and that I would wake up to the sound of Velcro each morning," Stephanie reflected. "Yet there I was, instead of hearing Velcro, I heard a knock on the door in its place."

The officers that arrived to pick up Stephanie only knew Jason was struck by a car and had severe brain injuries. They could offer her no comfort. They also couldn't allow her son to stay asleep in his bed, oblivious to the growing chaos. With no suspect in custody, there was no way to know if the incident was intentional. No way to tell if Jason's family was a target. They would all need to go to the hospital and Stephanie and her son would be offered protection until a suspect and a motive were identified.

Wrapped in a blanket in the back of a police cruiser, Stephanie watched the lights reflect off the driver's face, not knowing that just an hour earlier the same blue lights were flashing across her husband's while he lay on the ground unable to move or speak. Flashing blue lights would now reflect upon their lives and provide a greater source of pride than she knew possible.

The sense of brotherhood permeating the police organization is inexplicable. It exists because it's necessary. It's a sense of understanding, of sympathy and of protection. It's knowing someone who has walked a mile in your shoes will be by your side when you need it most. When an officer is injured or killed in the line of duty, this thin blue line is at its strongest and most pure. No one knows that more than a parent, sibling, spouse, or child of an officer upon arriving at a hospital where the officer has been brought. Shoulder to shoulder they stand, hoping to stave off the darkness for this family. If not forever, then maybe just long enough for them to say goodbye.

Stephanie met his line at the hospital. Officers, their spouses, and politicians had gathered. So many that an area of the emergency room needed to be sectioned off. An officer was down; a community would hold up the family.

While Stephanie felt many eyes upon her, she had only two goals – get her son out of town to safety and do everything she could to comfort Jason. While waiting for her parents to arrive and pick up her son, she wasn't able to see Jason; her son couldn't go into the room with her and he wouldn't let her leave him alone in the waiting room. Jason was stable, but he was not in good condition.

Stephanie's emotional condition wasn't much better than Jason's physical condition. Suddenly very alone, she tried to answer the multitude of medical history questions that were being asked, hide her grief from her son, and pray the man she loved would pull through and the nightmare would end.

Having been a part of the department only a year, neither Jason nor Stephanie had any strong relationships with the people there. Stephanie and the officers around her were thrown into a situation in which they could offer no meaningful comfort to each other. They could only exist in a surreal situation, trapped with their own thoughts. Try as they might, finding a way to connect with each other in the darkest of hours wasn't easy. Stephanie had their full support and they had her gratitude for offering it, yet both parties felt very alone and anxious.

Meanwhile, the manhunt for the person who hit Jason continued. With eye witness testimony, they had a good lead on the suspect. The suspect was somewhere roaming free, while Stephanie was on lockdown for her safety. For 14 hours she was isolated and Jason was a no-contact patient. This meant only Stephanie was allowed to know about his condition, and no one was allowed access to him or his information. They were insulated from the press and the public. Because of this, Stephanie had to stay at the hospital to make decisions. She simply couldn't leave; there was no one to take her place.

She felt very alone. Her child was in another town. Her husband was fighting for his life. A criminal was on the loose and no one had a motive yet. She was living with the threat of danger over her head in addition to everything else. It wouldn't be until the suspect was in custody that the threat was lifted.

By noon the next day, Stephanie needed a break. Jason was barely holding on. Stephanie was updating the crowd in the waiting room every 30-45 minutes on his condition; she was fighting a sinus infection, missing her son, and trying to make too many decisions with too little time. Four officers escorted her home to shower; although the suspect was now in custody, the officers cleared the house before they let her in and allowed her a few minutes of privacy. They were all shaken to the core and wanted to ensure the house was safe.

The officers who had escorted her were awkwardly holding their own. An officer was down; it could have been any one of them at that call. Their families were worried, they were emotionally wrought and they were now in the house of a woman who was in indescribable pain. They didn't know how to help her or themselves.

At what point do any of them have privacy? Every need of Stephanie's was being tended to; she simply had to think that she was thirsty and water appeared. She wasn't allowed to be alone. She had yet to cry. She wanted nothing more than to go back in time and make Jason change his words. She wanted to hear him say, "Always," but she knew it wouldn't have made a difference. It was just a silly superstition that so many LEO families hang their hopes on.

Stephanie and her four uniformed officers stopped at Walgreens on the way back to the hospital to pick up sinus medicine. This would be the first time of many that people would stop and look at Stephanie, this time out of curiosity – What had this woman done to need a four officer escort? Later she would be looked upon with pity and sometimes respect and other times fear. Fear that they, too, could be a family member of a dead officer.

Less than 24 hours had passed since Jason had been hit, but it felt like an eternity. Stephanie didn't want to call Jason's mother, Marsa, until she had more information. After being told they were in for a long haul and the next 48 hours would be critical, she now realized she had no choice but to call. Marsa was away on an RV camping trip in Maine, and her world was about to be shattered. Her oldest son was clinging to life and she was 2,200 miles away.

Marsa and her husband immediately began the drive to Texas. While her husband drove, Marsa looked for flights. Since they couldn't find an immediate flight, they continued the long drive hoping to find a flight somewhere along the way. By the time they reached Texas, Marsa would only have two hours with her son.

The evening of the 14th, another officer's wife, who happened to be an intensive care unit nurse, told Stephanie they needed to talk. No one wants to hear these words. Stephanie didn't want to talk; talking meant making decisions, decisions meant she could no longer deny what was going on, and reality meant Jason was dying.

Stephanie hadn't slept; the medication they gave her to help her relax didn't help. She was angry and wasn't talking to anyone. She closed herself in a room and made it clear the only person she wanted to see was Jason's mother.

A friend and fellow officer of Jason's tried to talk to Stephanie. They were worried about her. They weren't sure she understood what was happening and she really needed to make some difficult choices. Something he said reached her, and she realized that if she didn't start making decisions, the doctors would make them for her. The choices they made might not be the ones she could live with and she would regret it for the rest of her life.

Jason was lying in a bed, tubes everywhere; the swelling in his brain was fighting with his blood pressure. To alleviate the swelling in his brain, Jason needed to be elevated; however, when he was elevated, his blood pressure would drop. If the blood pressure went down, the swelling went up. If the swelling went down, the blood pressure went up. There was no solution to this that would save his life. He had only a few hours left.

Stephanie and Jason were a couple in love with their lives ahead of them, but they were also realistic. They knew that life could be fleeting. At any time either one of them could be gone. They had discussed the "what ifs" and they both understood each other's end of life desires. They didn't want to face them, but they understood. Knowing what Jason wanted offered Stephanie a small bit of comfort.

Marsa arrived the morning of June 15, 2013 to find that Jason was struggling to stay alive; he had stopped breathing on his own since she had last talked to Stephanie. It was a lot to take in. A mother seeing her young, healthy son struck down by a careless driver who was more concerned about getting out of a park than about the lives of those around him. Marsa was in such a state of shock she could barely speak.

The plan was to do a brainwave test at 6am; if he coded before then, they would not resuscitate. Stephanie looked to Marsa for approval to sign the "Do Not Resuscitate" (DNR) order; angry she had to make this decision, Stephanie's shaking hands signed the paperwork effectively telling Jason it was okay to let go.

Many people might say she signed up for it by marrying a cop. She didn't. None of us do. We sign up for hardship. They sign up for honor, love, and other reasons we may never understand. It's difficult to understand their sacrifice. When Stephanie signed the DNR, she understood it more clearly than ever. The moment she heard the pounding on their door and opened it to the uniformed officers standing on the other side at 12:40am her life was altered forever. She had no choice but to go in and say goodbye.

"Telling him to, 'Let go,' were some of the hardest words I have ever said," she recalled. "Yet, because my love for him was so strong, I knew that he would never want to live a life where he couldn't return to being a patrol officer. Letting him go was right by him."

While Jason's blood pressure dropped to zero, he was surrounded by his family telling him they loved him, they understood his sacrifice and they were proud of him. They took turns talking to him until the doctor came in and pronounced him dead at approximately 3:30am on June 15, 2013. It was 27 hours after he stood in a park telling an SUV to stop because it was going too fast.

Other people died that day, all around the country, but Jason died because he chose to put on a uniform and stand in a park to try to get everyone out safely so the neighbors could fall back asleep without the noise and commotion of a party. Had it not been for his choice to serve his community, he would not have been in the park and he might still be alive today. He chose his path. He chose to serve. He did not choose to die.

At 7am Jason was being transported to Dallas for an autopsy because this was now a murder investigation. Stephanie went home to take a break before he returned. Her house was already full of people and food.

No, she didn't want to take out pictures and look at him when he was alive. She didn't want anyone talking to her son when he arrived because she still hadn't figured out how she was going to tell him Daddy was gone. She also didn't want to think about "then" and "now." Her life would now be defined as *before* and *after*; there would be plenty of time to think about that.

In fact, how does one tell a 4 ½ year old their daddy went to work and isn't coming home? You tell them people make good and bad choices. That sometimes the bad choices are so bad you can't fix them. Daddy tried to get people to make good choices; that was his job. He tried to protect people and help the ones that make bad decisions. Daddy was struck by a car driven by someone who made a bad decision; the doctors tried to help him but they couldn't. Daddy isn't coming back.

Just as water appeared when Stephanie needed it, the funeral was put together according to her wishes. She wanted Jason to be buried at home, 1.5 hours away. No one gave a thought to how crazy the logistics were, they simply did it because that is what she wanted.

The Pine Bluff and Texarkana Police Departments participated; Jason received the funeral of a hero and his son noticed. He smiled at the gravesite and said, "My Daddy was a hero. Look at all the people that are here!"

His daddy was also always thinking of his son. Ninety minutes before the fateful call to the park, Jason had bragged about how he had just put a deposit on an XBOX for his son. Stephanie first heard about it during the eulogies that spoke of his courage, his dedication, and his love for his family.

It was bittersweet to see crowds of people honoring him in death when they should be supporting his profession in life. Stephanie was angry that people needed to be there; not angry at the people, at the reason. Jason was dead, and if Jason weren't dead all of them would be elsewhere. She was honored that so many people respected his profession and sacrifice enough to travel great distances to pay respect.

The eulogies and the crowds. More people than Stephanie had ever known in her lifetime. Enough business cards to light a bonfire. She and Jason had spent six years of their lives doing what they believed was honorable and respectful, serving their community as a police officer and a teacher, and it ended in death. She had a right to be angry, frustrated and confused.

Society needs heroes, but most policemen, firemen, and soldiers don't want to become heroes; they want to be men and women doing their jobs. They want to be supported and understood. Unfortunately, they find the most support and understanding when death comes in the line of duty. With death comes the onset of the hero label. With the hero title bestowed, everyone seems to know Jason. They won't ask for permission to speak at his funeral. They will simply do it because they know the person in the coffin would not be there if it weren't for a position that required them to give their lives for others. People who didn't know him spoke as if they did, and, while society was claiming its newest hero, Stephanie wanted to grieve alone. More than that, though, she wanted Jason back.

Stephanie's liaison officer from the department, who was Jason's lieutenant, was kind and sensed Stephanie's conflicting feelings. He gently reminded her that, "There will be thousands of people who want to bless you and your son; it's all they have to give you. They know they can't give you back your husband; if you resist them, you take away their ability to thank you for your sacrifice." It was at that moment Stephanie became acutely aware of the paradox of the police wife.

She must be humble and grateful; she had a role to play for Jason and his profession. Although what she was feeling inside was contrary to what was expected, in a way she belonged to society as a movie star belongs to their fans. She stood for hours shaking hands and hugging well-wishers, hearing generic statements that were meant to ease her pain but couldn't, making decisions to appease the people who wanted to grieve with her, and all the while the line of mourners kept getting longer.

Stephanie wasn't ungrateful. She was numb. When you live your life simply and are suddenly thrown into the spotlight, it becomes difficult to manage, understand, and cope. Being the center of attention because of a death brings a chaos that most people will never experience. Stephanie shared her husband, her grief, and her family with the public at the most private moment of her life. She knew that it was her responsibility as the wife of a public servant. For that, they thanked her.

On March 25, 2014, the trial of Justin Miles Sanders began. The sergeant on the scene described how he found Jason unconscious and bleeding from his ears. The jury heard from the 9-1-1 caller who reported seeing groups of people in the park fighting and smoking. They watched the dash cam video of Jason being hit, the passenger of the SUV looking at his body and then driving off. They heard the public defender say it was an accident and Sanders couldn't be held accountable. They found out that Sanders had tried to get around Jason because he had marijuana in his car, was dealing it, and was afraid of being caught.

Justin Sanders was effectively evading arrest. In doing so, he struck and killed a man. Although he continues to deny hitting Jason Sprague, he was charged with first degree murder.

Stephanie and Justin Sanders' mother were scheduled to speak during the punishment phase; this meant neither was allowed in the courtroom for the trial. After petitioning the court, an exception was made so Stephanie could sit through the trial; Justin Sanders' mother was also allowed to be there. Stephanie sat through two weeks of testimony, video, and photo reminders of what happened to her husband. She felt strongly about being part of the trial because she was the only physical remembrance of what was taken away from her family. She was afraid the jury wouldn't understand the emotional changes and the loss they had suffered, so she thought that a physical reminder of who Jason was would help.

Sanders' attorney was granted a change of venue, and that put Stephanie in a hotel, two hours from home, surrounded by the people who witnessed her husband's death, many of whom simply didn't want to be there. Rather than go home to the physical and emotional safety of her own bed, she was surrounded by the "us versus them" mentality. The police and their supporters, and the people who were afraid they would be cited for being in the park that night and smoking pot.

What was far worse was that Sanders was out on bail; Stephanie ran into him in the halls, the waiting rooms, and restaurants. He was free to move about and live his life while her husband was dead. Her son was starting a difficult emotional journey and she was just trying to make it through the day. At one point, he held a door open for her. She refused to go through it. The anger and the hypocrisy of it all was too much. It was too late for him to be a gentleman.

Stephanie would not leave the trial, no matter how many times she had to listen to the audio after Jason was hit. She knew she was sacrificing her mental well-being, but she knew she had to stay. She had to remind the jury there was a wife and child left behind. So much had already been taken away; she wasn't going to leave, she wasn't going to walk out or cry. She was going to hold it together for Jason.

"I've spent more of my time replaying evidence over and over in my mind, and analyzing Jason's last moments," she recalled softly. "Yes, I sat through that rear dash cam video more than once. I promise you, I still don't know how I did it. I wonder if the message my presence during the video sent to the jury was worthy enough of the years I'll spend replaying those last few moments in my head."

It took the jury less than eight hours to reach a guilty verdict.

The paradox reared its head again. It was a bittersweet moment: a 21-year-old kid was sentenced to 30 years in prison, and by the time he was eligible for parole her own son would be 20. Stephanie watched as a mother cried and mourned the loss of her child. A mother who truly believed her son was innocent beyond a shadow of a doubt. One family was crying because they lost their son, another family was crying because justice was served.

Stephanie was seeing beyond her pain. Sanders had no previous record, and anyone can make a stupid mistake. She was seeing the other mother's pain and she began a new battle within herself. She watched his mother say goodbye before he was led away. "You could almost feel sorry when you look into his eyes and see the reality of his choices sink in. I'm angry because these emotions feel as if they are a betrayal of Jason's sacrifice to his brothers/sisters in blue. In fact, I have debated sharing such emotions because I was afraid people wouldn't understand why I feel them," Stephanie said.

Was she betraying Jason's memory by feeling sorry for their family? No. She was letting go of her anger. She was choosing grace. She was choosing to become a person Jason would be proud of.

Being that person comes at a cost, though, and the cost hurt. She had to survive taking their son to his first soccer game in the very same park his daddy was killed. A son who has an entire lifetime of firsts to live without Jason: first days of school, first dates, first time driving. Stephanie has lived through her year of firsts, but their son's grief journey was just beginning.

Widowed at 30, Stephanie lost friends because they didn't know what to say, and others felt badly about talking about their husbands in front of her. Society doesn't have a lot of room for young widows. She wasn't shunned, far from it. Her community rallied around her and showered her with love. She is "blessed beyond measure with officers, their families, and community member who make sure that we live as normal of a life as possible. We still stand in awe at the amount of community support we have been shown."

In private, they are still a broken family trying to find where they will now fit. Her son couldn't sleep through the night for a time because he was afraid someone would kill his mother, too. Stephanie has nightmares and the sounds from the funeral haunt her at night. The 21-gun salute that honored his sacrifice now startles her awake in a cold sweat. The front door to her home has become a symbol to be dreaded, for by opening it that night she let death into her home.

In June 2015, they moved back to Arkansas. Stephanie feels it's time for this phase of their life to be over. Although their community has embraced her, it's a constant reminder of Jason. She can't move on with her life when everyone knows who she is. When she goes out to dinner, she isn't necessarily thinking of Jason's death, but when she sees the looks of the faces on the people around her, she is reminded that they can look away and go back to their dinner. She can't. She and her son deserve to have a good day. To eat dinner without feeling pitied. To talk to someone without having to be "the officer's widow."

Despite wanting to see Jason, the man, not Jason, the officer, she will always be an advocate for policemen and their families. Since Jason's death, Stephanie feels she has a new calling in life to fulfill. She doesn't want people to avoid the difficult law enforcement discussions around her because of who she is; she wants to be able to choose to participate. Choose to be happy, to speak up and to prove her husband's sacrifice was worth something.

Stephanie and every other member of law enforcement around the world want you to know that it's not the number of deaths you should be counting. It's the way in which the lives are taken that counts. It's the belief that two ounces of drugs are worth more than a human life. It's the idea that the police put your child in prison, when, in reality, your child puts himself in prison with the choices he made. Those are the things we should be counting — the number of times we blame the police for our own shortcomings.

Some LEO families live from one vacation or milestone to the next: "I hope he doesn't get injured or killed around Christmas," or "God forbid he has to be injured or killed, but let it be near a school vacation so the kids can cope without missing too much school and adding that to their setbacks." They are relieved they made it to the next turn of the calendar. Jason's son won't live with that worry, because he won't live with his father.

His son is now six years old, and over the last six months he's started showing symptoms of the trauma. He's just now noticing what it's like to not have a daddy; he sees other dads with his friends and often says that Jason plays with him because he's in his heart. He wants to keep hearing about the accident and why his daddy couldn't be saved. He's trying to process it as best a child can. Why didn't Daddy stay in the car? Why didn't someone shoot the car before he got hit?

Jason's son finds solace in constellations; he learned how ships use them as navigation points from Jason. He believes his daddy has chosen the Big Dipper to build his mansion in heaven. At night he lies in bed and tells Jason about his day, blowing kisses to heaven and asking his daddy to visit him in his dreams. He's not an angry boy; his mother never burdened him with her emotions. He is simply a boy being raised into a man who understands the value of sacrifice and willingness to pay the true cost if needed.

SANTOS

Santos' story is long and difficult, much like the road ahead of him. Because of a drunk driver, his life has become a constant battle for benefits and dignity. His name is not memorialized anywhere, his story was not sensationalized; he is simply a police officer who became a paraplegic on the evening of June 10, 2012. He is one of many officers left behind once they become critically injured; after the fundraisers are over people return to their lives, jobs and families. It's no one's fault, it's just the way it is.

Santos fell in love with policing when he was a young boy. His father served warrants in Chicago's toughest neighborhoods for 18 years and his brother has been a Chicago cop for 26 years. Santos fondly remembers the days his father let him ride along with him when he put on his three piece suit and served warrants.

"I thought it was so awesome that my dad didn't have a hair out of place. I also thought that the police station was the coolest place ever. I wanted to be just like him. The two coolest jobs in the world were playing in the NFL or being a cop. I became a cop."

It would take six interviews before Santos would land a job in Indianapolis. He took his then girlfriend Fran with him on the sixth interview as a good luck charm. It worked. On April 30, 2007, he started the police academy and, "loved every minute of it. Sometimes I wish I could go back because that's how much fun I had despite the fact that it was the hardest thing I ever did."

Santos and Fran married on a Florida beach in July 2008, after he graduated the academy and had a chance to settle into his new job. On a day when the temperature hit 100 degrees, Fran's two boys and Santos' daughter stood by them to bear witness to their love. They would quickly add two more children to their family for a total of five children.

On the morning of June 10, 2012, Santos and Fran were cleaning up after their son's tenth birthday party. A few of his friends had slept over and before Santos' shift started, he greeted parents at the door to their apartment while they picked up their kids. Once everyone had gone home, Santos headed into work, their 17-year-old son went to a friend's house and Fran stayed home with the other kids ages 15, 10, 3 and 18 months.

Fran napped on the couch with the baby around 7pm when Santos was dispatched to a call reporting an erratic driver. Jerrel Watkins, drunk, sped through a stop sign at 50mph slamming into Santos' cruiser. The impact spun the cruiser in a counter clockwise direction. A Ford F250 struck him head-on reversing the spin. The impact threw Santos out his passenger window from the driver seat. Only a block from the scene, he had just unbuckled his seat belt in anticipation of exiting his vehicle.

Fran woke from her nap to the sound of the phone ringing. She didn't recognize the number, so she didn't answer. The caller didn't leave a message. A few minutes later the same number called again; this time there was a message. Santos' sergeant asked Fran to return his call right away.

"I'm a pacer. When I talk on the phone, I pace. I laid the baby down and began pacing. Honestly, my mind never registered that something bad had happened. I don't know what I was thinking, I wasn't panicking, but I knew that sergeants don't call for no reason."

This sergeant's first time ever calling anyone about a critical incident, his nervousness was obvious to Fran. He seemed panicked and rambling, as if he didn't know what to say.

"He introduced himself and asked me if I remembered him. He talked about where we had met and about our kids. Then he told me that there's been an accident, that Santos was breathing and conscious but I needed to come to the hospital. I remember sitting on the bed then. I never sit when I talk on the phone. He offered to send someone to come get me but I said no. I don't know why, but I said no."

Fran and Santos were new to Indianapolis, knew very few people and Fran had no idea how to get to the hospital. She spent the next few minutes worrying about what to do, wondering why she declined the ride, wondering how she would get there and what she would do with the kids.

Rational decision making isn't easy when someone you love is injured, even when you don't know the extent. Fran did the best she could, she remembered meeting the neighbor in the apartment below her, the woman with the young children, and hoped she could give Fran a ride.

Her neighbor quickly agreed, and Fran called her oldest son, "I need you to come home, Dad's been in an accident. I need you to sit home with your brothers and sisters while I go to the hospital."

As soon as her son arrived, Fran left with her neighbor. Although Fran wasn't panicked and had no idea how badly Santos was hurt, her neighbor became very nervous about getting Fran to her injured husband. The neighbor lived in Indianapolis her entire life but in her haste, she couldn't remember how to get to the hospital. They kept getting off and on the highway with the neighbor's young children in the back and Fran's phone constantly ringing. Why she wasn't at the hospital yet? After the third call, Fran began to panic.

The fiancé of Santos' Field Training Officer (FTO) was a local sheriff. She told Fran to pull the car over, walk to the nearest intersection and read the street signs to her. Within minutes the sheriff arrived. Perhaps subconsciously, Fran delayed getting in the patrol car. Her neighbor was crying because she had failed. Fran stood on the corner hugging and comforting her until the sheriff put her in the car and whisked her away.

"When we pulled up to the ambulance bay, I don't know what went through my head. There were about 50 officers outside and they all started heading toward me. I locked the car door and stared straight ahead. I wasn't getting out of that car. They didn't tell me on the phone that it was serious. No one said it was critical. With all of those officers around, I knew it was bad. I refused to get out."

The sheriff used her PA system to clear the ambulance bay noticing they spooked Fran. She appeared to be in shock. All but two FTO's moved inside. They approached the car and gently knocked on the window.

"Fran, we need you to get out of the car. Santos needs you right now. Please come with us."

Slowly, she did. Hundreds of officers, wives, and chaplains, packed the hospital hallway.

"I kept wondering why all of these people were here. Didn't he just break his leg or hit his head? Why are all these people here for a broken leg? I didn't understand why everyone was hugging me and grasping my hand."

Fran can't tell you if she was in denial, shock, or both. She backed herself against the wall, stood perfectly still and didn't speak to anyone until the nurse came to get her.

"When you see your husband, you will see a huge hematoma on his head. It's just a big pocket of blood. It's nothing to worry about; it's not life-threatening. It just looks terrible, but it's nothing," reassured the nurse.

The hematoma was one of the last things Fran saw when she was led into the room. There was too much going on. An officer was trying to get Santos' statement, medical staff were tending to Santos' battered body and Santos was pissed off. Matt, his FTO, stood by his bedside hoping to offer Santos some comfort.

"Stop pushing me down! I need to get up! Why can't I get up?! What have you done to me? I don't know why I can't get off this gurney. I don't know why none of you people don't care that there is a drunk out there and he is going to kill someone! I'm the only one who can stop him! Why doesn't anyone else care?"

Santos appeared to be looking right through his FTO as he told Santos, "You got him. You stopped him, and he's in custody. You don't have to get up. Just lie down and rest."

Still agitated, Santos replied, "I don't know why I can't get up!"

"They just want to check you out."

"I don't want to be here!"

Matt needed to keep talking to him to keep Santos calm. Fran could do nothing but look on.

"A young doctor kept running a pen along Santos' foot telling him to move his toes; Santos felt nothing and his toes weren't moving. I kept wondering why they were doing that. It still hadn't registered with me. It was like an out of body experience, like I wasn't a participant. I was simply on the edge watching everything."

Santos was rushed to the ICU while Fran and the two FTO's were put in a triage room to wait. Shortly thereafter, three doctors entered: the trauma doctor on duty and two residents.

Blunt and matter of fact, the trauma doctor asked Fran, harshly, "Are you the wife?"

She shook her head.

"Obviously you know what's going on?"

"No."

"You have no idea?"

He was irritated with her.

"Your husband was in an accident and has multiple life threatening injuries. Obviously his back is broken and he will never walk again."

As she began to fall backward, she remembers the officers grabbing her arms to steady her.

"Ma'am, do you understand what I am saying to you? Your husband will never walk again."

"No."

"What's no? What don't you understand?"

He looked to the FTO's, "She needs to understand, her husband will never walk again."

Fran continued to deny it. The doctors left the room leaving the FTO's confused and unsure what to do. Fran simply wasn't responding.

They felt it was best to take her to the family room for privacy and to determine what was next.

"As I walked down the hallway, it felt like the Green Mile. Everyone was crying, praying, and reaching for me. I kept wondering, 'What is wrong with these people?' The next thing I knew the hospital chaplain stopped me and he was over the top praying. He was so over the top praying and consoling me that I looked to the FTOs and said, 'He just died.'"

The chaplain appeared so grief stricken that the FTO's also thought Santos had died.

"We were just with him. How can he be dead?"

The chaplain explained Santos wasn't dead, he was just praying fervently for him. They quickly pushed past the chaplain and brought Fran into the room where the medical team took over. They walked Fran through everything. They notified both sets of parents and sent a patrol car to pick up Santos' mother and drive her the 3 hours to Indianapolis to ensure she didn't hurt herself on the way down.

Santos wasn't stable enough for surgery. Although the medical staff told him what was going on, he was also in shock. Between the trauma to his body, the shock, and narcotics for the pain, he didn't know where he was. He spent twelve days in the ICU. During the last few days, he would have moments of extreme lucidity, but when the doctors tried to talk to him about his condition, he would disengage. He simply wasn't ready to face it.

There was no preparation for rehabilitation after the ICU. Santos was sent into a process which was physically invasive, mortifying and emotionally devastating. After seeing him fall asleep during physical therapy because he was overmedicated and hearing his objections to the way he was being handled, Fran realized she needed to accept what was happening and begin to work toward healing.

"I realized I needed to stay strong for my family, my kids and Santos. I needed to start fixing things and the first thing I did was get Santos the proper medication. Once he stabilized, it started to hit him. He realized he couldn't do the things they were asking him to do. There was a lot of emotion – denial, anger and wondering 'why me?'"

At first Santos would refuse to learn things, "This is ridiculous," he'd say. "I don't need to learn that. I'm not paralyzed! I'm walking out of here."

Fran convinced him to learn it, "for now." He may not need it long-term. He may just need it for a few months; they'd do it together. Santos agreed, on the surface. At physical therapy, whenever a person learned a new skill, they were supposed to ring the bell. Santos refused. He said he'd only ring the bell when he could walk again. He spent six weeks in rehabilitation and never touched the bell.

While Santos was adjusting to his new body and lifestyle Fran was also adjusting. She was learning to be a nurse and caregiver to the man she loved. In doing so, she kept a close eye on him for any changes in his body or mood. One day, Fran noticed a small abrasion on his back. She was told it was nothing to worry about and that it would heal on its own. It did not heal and Santos' health started to decline. He was dying.

The small sore turned into a pressure ulcer which developed four infections – MRSA, VRE, E Coli and staphylococcus. It traveled to his bone and manifested itself as bone osteomyelitis. Literally, his bones were rotting in his body. He became very ill, couldn't eat and became incoherent. The smell from his wound became unbearable and Fran was not receiving support from Santos' case manager. At her wits end, she took pictures of the wound, sent it to a few friends and asked what they thought she should do.

Within 30 minutes officers and friends arrived at their door to help, they took Santos to the ER near their apartment. Unequipped to handle a case like his, Santos' condition was too severe for treatment. They were able to find a wound care surgeon who saw him the next day. The surgeon was furious; Santos was near death and he couldn't understand why someone hadn't treated him sooner. After eight hours of surgery to remove his entire tailbone and clean up the infections, which included 11 blood transfusions, Santos spent five months in the hospital. He was released in December 2012.

In 2013, Santos saw more hospitalizations and the day he could finally see Jerrel Watkins in court. Watkins had a blood-alcohol level of .29 when he got behind the wheel of his car and hit Santos. With his wife, father and brother beside him, Santos listened as Watkins received the maximum sentence – 3 years. In reality, he would serve only 368 days behind bars while Santos spends the rest of his life in a wheelchair no longer able to chase his children in the yard.

February 2014 brought the most devastating news of all. The entire family had the flu but Santos wasn't getting any better. Fran took him to the ER only to be sent home because no one saw what was building in his body. Three weeks later, after an MRI, the surgeon saw something shocking. The osteomyelitis was back and it had eaten up Santos' spine. His back was broken much worse than it had been at the time of the accident.

Because the hardware in Santos' body was infected, it all had to be removed and replaced. This couldn't happen until his body was infection free. He had to lie on his back for 30 days without the hardware. During this stay, a series of complications, many of them life-threatening afflicted him. It was one thing after another. He was fused from head to toe with double rods and screws.

Despite the physical and emotional set-backs, Santos was determined to return to work. Assigned desk duty, he was able to serve his community from his wheel chair. He believed that one day he would walk again. In March 2014, the city had an automobile specially outfitted so he could drive himself to and from work.

In June 2014, less than two months after returning to work, Santos was readmitted to the hospital. Lying on his back for so long had caused another sore which kept him in the hospital for the next nine months.

Meanwhile, Jerrel Watkins was about to be arrested for another DUI. He had been released from probation on February 2, 2014, having completed all of the legally required punishment for paralyzing Santos. At this time, he is still in prison for his new offense, serving more time for his second DUI than for the accident that nearly killed Santos.

Three years, 24 surgeries later, Santos finally returned home in May 2015. Santos required one surgery to fuse his spine because of the accident. The others were due to complications.

The accident didn't only affect Santos, his entire family was affected. His wife Fran became depressed. She would get the kids out the door in the morning then come home and cry and eat and stay in bed. Trudging through the day, she couldn't wait to go back to bed. She was finally treated for PTSD but she hasn't fully recovered. She probably never will.

"Honestly, I think I struggle with a lot of anger. I don't know what I'm angry about, I get agitated easily. I hate that I've become like that. There is depression but I don't know what I am depressed about. I don't have time for any of it. I have to repress it as best as I can because of the kids," she said matter-of-factly. "There is no help. We have no family here and everyone has lives to get back to. I remember the chief telling me that they'd be there for us for life. I thought, 'No they won't. They have kids and wives and jobs and have to move on. We are on our own.' We've relied on strangers and a few friends to survive.

"In the beginning, it was easier; our department does have a Police Officer Support Team (POST). If there is a death or critical incident, the POST assembles. We were assigned a POST member, someone we had never met before, but he was with me 24/7 for the first two weeks. A meal train was set up so that there were three meals per day at home and the kids were constantly receiving gifts." Fran laughs as she explains how things happened; she tends to do that when she gets nervous or upset, and it's a better alternative than crying. "In the beginning it was mind-blowing and amazing – the generosity and taking care of your own. No one wanted for anything for the first 4-6 weeks; errands were done and clean clothes were available. Everything. The auxiliary rallied as well. They helped with planning and fundraising. It was amazing. The problem was that you were trying to deal with the incident and your feelings while they made sure everything else was done. It gives you a false sense of security; you think that you will always have people around and be taken care of. It's not true. Once everything settles down, you are left alone to try to pick up the pieces and it's very hard."

Picking up the pieces for herself and Santos was difficult; trying to hold the kids together was more complicated. Each child has been affected profoundly and differently. Their voices haunt Santos.

"I miss you and I don't want to leave you."

"It's like you're dead when you leave and go to the hospital. We never get to see you."

Santos and Fran now have a son who will always remember his father was paralyzed the day after his tenth birthday. A daughter who regressed after the accident and now suffers from separation anxiety; she became introverted and didn't want to talk to anyone. Daddy's little girl has missed her daddy. A child with ADHD that has become extremely loyal to family and very empathetic. He went into mother hen mode, trying to take care of everyone but ate his finger nails off and tore nervous holes in his shirt trying. The stress became too much.

Other children have distanced themselves because the entire situation has become too much. As young adults, they could separate themselves physically and emotionally from a situation that was too overwhelming.

The money they saved for their home is now gone; bills ate it. Medical equipment and emotions now crowd the patient loving home they once knew. And whenever Santos has a doctor's appointment, Daddy's little girl panics and worries that he won't come home.

For the children too young to escape, they see and feel Santos' pain daily. It's hard to be in middle school with a behavioral disorder; it's even harder when your father is in a wheelchair, and it gives the other kids one more thing to pick on you about. Caring for and about his family is more important so he copes and tries not to worry his parents.

While his children and wife adjust to their lives, Santos struggles with the challenges of his situation. Santos was kept on his department's payroll because he had every intention of returning to work after his accident and, between hospital visits, he did. His schedule necessitated independence; he couldn't rely on people to take time out of their day to take him where he needed to be. Oftentimes, his needs were unpredictable. As Santos has no control over his lower body, he has put his dignity on the line. He has to freshen himself up at inopportune times. His career meant so much to him that he was willing to withstand the humiliation.

In February 2015, while in the hospital, Santos was asked to medically retire. His state doesn't have social security and he was offered 60% of his current salary. Like Michael in South Carolina, Santos is currently fighting for legislation. Santos learned of the imbalance and how many departments don't offer officers full benefits when they are permanently disabled on duty. Retire healthy, you receive full benefits. Die, the family receives full benefits. Get injured on duty, you barely get enough to survive.

For officers like Santos, the frustration is overwhelming. Their car is their office, just like animal control, EMS and firefighters. Being injured by a drunk driver, or any other scenario, should be recognized with full benefits. "Why do we get kicked to the curb and overlooked when we survived? We have to struggle with being the unwanted red-headed stepchild while other families are taken care of financially and spiritually. It's as if we were never part of the force. We've got to get that to change somehow, someway."

Throughout his ordeal, Santos has found there are many issues to champion. He wants people to know that police are human; he'd like more accountability for drunk drivers whether they are wearing the uniform or not and most importantly, he'd like people to know what happens to an officer when they become injured.

"It's hard to get anyone to document we are all human. We all bleed the same issues, we all have kids, and we bleed red. I took an oath to protect people whether they are going to spit on me or not, but I don't want them to cast me aside because I am doing my job. Don't look at me differently. I'm no different than the electrician or the plumber. There's always going to be someone bad out there. There are bad officers out there. But we aren't all bad."

Regarding police who drink and drive, "How can I be above the law and go arrest someone that did the same thing the next day? That's a credibility issue. It's a choice you made to do that. We don't always have to run to alcohol. That's what the old-timers used to do. You can't let alcohol over take you; find a hobby, read a bible, and build an airplane. Nothing says you have to have beer or wine. Enjoy it but do it the right way. Don't abuse it and don't get behind the wheel. You're going to get a 32oz beer? This is a choice. You should set up something so you have a ride.

"If the public is going to hold us to a higher standard, we need to hold ourselves to a higher standard. We took an oath to protect people. We did. Joe Blow down the street didn't hold us to that standard we decided to do it. We are not better but we need to hold ourselves better. We need to act better."

Santos is also hopeful and steadfast in his belief things will change. "I will walk again but just not at this moment. There's just something in my faith. I believe I will. Fran and I have had some tough times; we talk to each other honestly. We try to let go of our anger. She's done so much for me; I've got a good wife.

"I honestly believe that I got this job because of my wife because she is a positive person and God knew she could handle it. She is the strongest part of me. She is my rock, and sometimes I don't think I could have gotten through some of this without her."

Fran knows how Santos feels and she knows what her role has become.

"Keeping Santos alive is a full time job. I don't think he fully grasps how many times he has died. I've become hyper-vigilant. I understand how serious things are and I need to make sure he also understands. There is only so much he can do so I am here to help him with the rest. We've been told he has no brain damage but he has no memory of the accident. He'll never get it back because of the double concussion.

"We had to figure out how to maneuver based on the initial accident. Now there is a new struggle daily because of the complications. It just seems to go on forever.

"I have to be his advocate; I have to tell people what he needs all the time. No more sunshine and rainbows. I always come in guns blazing. I've had to become the person I never wanted to become. I question everything. It's something I have to do. Who is going to carry the ball if I fall apart? My job 24/7 is to keep Santos alive. If something happens to him, I don't know what will happen to me."

CODY

Take a look around you, who do you see? Your husband, wife, son, daughter or friend? What do you love most about them? The gleam in their eye, sense of humor or their laugh? What if all of that changed in an instant? What if their face changed, they could no longer cry and the single effort of speaking exhausted them? What if your friendships became distance memories and you have to learn to love a new person?

Cody and his family know how that feels all too well; his life was changed by an accident that was caused by a sequence of events over which he had little control. An accident is defined as an unfortunate event resulting especially from carelessness or ignorance. On January 13, 2011, carelessness and ignorance caused Cody's accident.

At 5:30pm the Blytheville Police Department received a call reporting an alleged armed robbery. When officers arrived on the scene, Chris Wamble told police that he had been hit in the head with a gun and robbed of $4,000. After providing the officers with a description of the suspects and their vehicle, it was broadcast by the police dispatcher. After only a few minutes, Arkansas State Police identified the vehicle and alerted the other units in the area. Believing the officers were in pursuit of armed and potentially dangerous suspects, Cody turned on his lights and sirens and sped toward the location to assist.

Another car was on the road that day, a car that had pulled over when the first police car passed. Perhaps the driver didn't see or hear Cody approaching; perhaps she thought she had enough time to cross the road and turn into the subdivision. Whatever the reason, she pulled back onto the two lane highway. It was the second decision that day that would redefine Cody's life.

As Cody approached the car, it made an unexpected move which caused Cody to swerve, hit a median and lose control of his cruiser. The front end of his cruiser became airborne, came down on black ice, slid another 70 feet and went into a drainage ditch. Cody remembers none of this, it was captured on his dashcam. As a matter of fact, Cody can't remember anything after New Year's Eve, 13 days earlier.

Cody and JT had very different upbringings; Cody was raised by his parents with his brother in a stable and loving home. His mother, Stephanie, says he was the perfect son – never in trouble, active, always checking in and very dependable. He felt that he was instilled with good morals and a desire to do the right thing.

Although JT was also a good kid, he's had his share of heartache. In 1994, under a lot of pressure at home and at work, JT's father shot himself wearing his police uniform. Adding to his devastation, JT found his father's body. These bloody images would stay with him forever. As if one suicide wasn't enough, JT's Grandfather also took his own life at the age of 82. He was old, sick and wanted things to end on his terms, choosing the same route as his son.

Cody and JT had wanted to become police officers for different reasons. Cody had become a member of the Blytheville emergency squad, a volunteer emergency services that responded to car accidents. He fell in love with policing and his desire to help people fit well with the profession.

For JT, it was a way for him to connect with his dad, a way to fill his memory with something other than the sight of his dead body. Although he remembers listening to Garth Brooks with his father, and continues to enjoy those memories today, he defines his father as a policeman and those memories are the strongest. Their bond was severed at too young an age and police work gave JT a way to feel connected to the father he loved.

By 2011, JT and Cody had firmly established themselves in their chosen careers but they were again heading down different paths. JT was becoming more and more affected by the job; soft-hearted and compassionate, he found the child abuse cases difficult. As a survivor of child abuse, he put everything he had into them and it was beginning to affect him. His strong sense of understanding what the victims experienced also gave him a feeling of unfinished business. He knew putting the perpetrators in jail didn't always bring closure; the victims' memories remain with them. Carrying the baggage of his victims was beginning to wear him down.

Meanwhile, Cody loved traffic work and was especially adept at spotting drunken drivers. He planned to join the State Police and spend his career there. Everything Cody did revolved around police work; he saw a future full of promise and hadn't become jaded by the job. He couldn't foresee anything stopping him from retiring from police work in his old age.

These two young men whose families had know each other all their lives were about to change profoundly. Their families were close, attended the same high school and worked for the same police department; they were good friends. After the accident, they became the best of friends.

According to Cody's mother, "That accident did something to all those young boys. We've never had an officer hurt like that and they all went down into that ditch."

At the time of the 9-1-1 call, no one knew that Wamble was lying, that he hadn't been robbed or that the car and suspects he described were of a vehicle that just happened to drive by while he was on the phone with the dispatcher. JT was finishing up another call and heard the information over the radio; everything seemed routine. As he headed to the location of the suspect vehicle, his adrenaline was pumping as usual and he prepared himself for what might happen next. His sense of routine quickly turned to dread as he heard someone say, "Are you okay? Stay with me. We are going to get you through this. You are going to be okay." The first officer on scene unknowingly had his microphone on. JT immediately thought, "I hope it's not Cody, I need to get to Cody." When he arrived on scene and saw another officer in the ditch, JT was overwhelmed with dread; he now knew for sure that the person in trouble was Cody.

On that cold, snowy afternoon in waist deep freezing water JT looked into Cody's squad car and wondered if he were still alive. His heart fell into his stomach; he was scared, sad and shocked. The cold water was quickly numbing his legs and he felt frozen – emotionally and physically. Knowing he would not be able to help if he acknowledged that it was Cody, he starting checking off a list in his head as if it were just another accident. He forced his training to kick in; he tried to elicit a response from Cody. There was none, dread was quickly starting to creep up on JT. Cody appeared to be barely hanging on.

Because of the location of the vehicle, the ambulance couldn't get to Cody. Although it was less than an hour, it seemed like hours for JT and the other officers working to get Cody out of the car. They had to rig a spine board to the side of the bridge and lower it down to the river to bring him up. By then a crowd had gathered and all were wondering if this young officer was going to make it. After safely extracting Cody, he was taken to the hospital where he was life-flighted to Memphis.

JT headed directly to the hospital stopping only to change his wet clothing. When he removed his pants, they were so frozen they stood on their own in the car port. He had frostbite and couldn't feel one of his feet for a week. None of that mattered, he didn't want medical attention. He didn't want to go to the station for a debriefing; all he could think about was getting to his friend and making sure he didn't die.

While on his way, JT called Kenny, Cody's father to let him know that Cody was in grave danger. JT didn't think that Cody would survive the trip to the hospital but he didn't want to sound frantic. He wanted to believe that there was a chance that Cody would survive; he wanted to give Cody's mother Stephanie hope.

When Stephanie heard that one of her children was in the hospital, she assumed it was her other son Clayton. She knew Cody's shift was ending in twenty minutes and he was probably at the station. She couldn't imagine what Clayton could have done to cause a serious injury. When she realized it was Cody, she expected the worst. She had been expecting the worst when at the age of twenty-one, he was a sworn officer carrying a gun. She had always been afraid that someone would hurt him, but she didn't expect a car accident to end his career.

Arriving at the hospital, JT and the family found Cody's external damage was not nearly as bad as his internal damage; broken bones, fractured ribs, eye damage and other as yet to be discovered injuries forced doctors to put Cody in a medically-induced coma for weeks. No one seemed sure if he was going to make it and if he did, how his brain would be affected.

Immediately following the accident JT took four days off work to sit by his friend; others volunteered their time so that there would be an officer with Cody 24 hours a day, 7 days a week. It was their way to support Cody and his family. In addition to the physical and emotional support, Cody's community held a fundraiser for him; medical bills were quickly mounting and his family didn't know how they were going to manage. They certainly didn't have the emotional capacity to cope with everything that was happening. Paying the bills was the least of their worries.

For thirty days, Cody lay in a coma. As often happens when a first responder is injured, there were lines of people waiting to see him, to show their concern. Stephanie distinctly remembers, "A large young man with dreadlocks, he came in to see Cody and he was crying." He was used to seeing Cody around his neighborhood and hearing Cody say, "Hey Mario, just checking to make sure you are okay." He missed the young officer who looked out for him and worried that he might not have someone checking in on him again.

Cody' parents heard stories they had never heard before; Cody was an officer that went about his business, didn't brag to his parents and didn't believe in airing other people's dirty laundry by sharing what happened on his shift. He also didn't want his mother to worry if she knew some of the things he had to deal with. Stephanie now knew what he did every day, she heard about some of the dangers he had faced and she met many of the people he had helped. For the first time since Cody became a police officer, Stephanie realized just how much Cody loved his job. She knew that when he woke up, he would want to get right back to work, but it wouldn't be that easy.

Cody awoke from his coma thirty days after the accident in a hospital room surrounded by family with no memory of what happened and unable to speak. Cody had extensive damage to the frontal lobe of his brain, the part of his brain that controls emotions, personality, motor function, memory, language, social behavior, impulse control, judgment and language. The frontal lobe controls most of our behavior and damage to it can be severe and wide-reaching. Unfortunately, Cody's damage required him to relearn everything he knew.

Cody would spend the next 30 months on a ventilator, endure months of painful physical therapy, and face surgeries to repair damage to other parts of his body. Walking, talking, and even breathing on his own became goals he hadn't needed to reach since he was a baby. He would spend months in pain relearning these skills.

He was also emotionally numb; because of the damage to his brain, Cody now had difficulty feeling emotion. Trying to explain it to others is difficult. It's as if someone flipped a switch and created a great chasm of apathy in Cody's mind. He knows he cares, but he can't feel it the way he had in the past. He can no longer cry, he knows that what is happening is sad or he can see someone else's pain but he can no longer experience it normally. For someone who has experienced so little of life and love, losing the ability to feel is devastating.

Cody spent a lot of time observing his family and friends as they came in and out; he wondered what was going through their minds and how they were able to cope with what had been happening to them. He often felt like a blank slate watching a story unfold. His friend JT was there to try to help him understand. JT visited Cody frequently in Memphis and Atlanta; he helped raise money for Cody's expenses, organized a prayer circle, and brought him mementos from the Atlanta Police Department to help cheer him in rehab. The first time JT visited Cody in Atlanta was also the first time JT had seen Cody awake since the accident. Not only was he awake, he was standing. JT broke down, completely overwhelmed with the feeling that Cody was going to make it. Their prayers had been answered.

During Cody's time in the Memphis and Atlanta hospitals, his father promised to shave the bread he had worn for the last thirty years when he heard Cody speak again. It was his way of coping with the events. Sometimes we don't know how to cope so we find a comfort zone; shaving a beard was a means to a goal. Cody worked for weeks with his speech therapist to be able to mutter the simple words, "Pop, shave." When he did, his family was overcome with emotion because they saw their son making his way back to them. While they cried and rejoiced, Cody looked on knowing the importance of the occasion but unable to fully express his happiness.

When Cody was finally able to return home, he was met with a police escort. JT was on duty and Cody got on the radio to let JT know he was 10-42, ending his shift and heading home. The shift Cody was about to begin would be the most difficult one yet.

"It's a very hard thing to witness, to see such a young person, someone you grew up with, played football with, change so dramatically," JT said.

When an officer, or anyone is injured, the initial outpouring of support can be overwhelming; everyone is at the ready taking care of the family, visiting and keeping their plight in the forefront of the community. After time, people return to their lives and find there isn't as much time for caregiving outside their immediate family. It's no one's fault, it's simply the way it is. There are only so many hours in the day, so much room for emotion. When Cody returned from the hospital, he had another groundswell of support and then people began to fade back to their normal lives. JT couldn't walk away.

JT is the kind of person that pours his heart into everything he does; as an officer, he never lost a child abuse case. He remembers every case; he understands the need for justice and reparation. He knows that the hurt doesn't go away when the case is closed. He also knows the victims suffer long after the doors to the courtroom close. He knew that Cody's injuries were going to cause him the same sort of suffering and he was ready to help.

Recovering from a knee injury and not knowing whether or not he could be returned to active duty, JT knew some of what Cody was experiencing. Cody was having a hard time understanding why he couldn't get right back to work; he didn't even consider that he may never return. He assumed he would. The police department offered him a sense of hope, letting him know a desk job would be available when he was ready. But his doctors were telling him otherwise.

Because Cody's reasoning had been affected by his brain injury, Cody may not have fully understood how damaged he had become. He didn't quite know the life he had lived so far wasn't coming back. He has a gift for masking his feelings; outwardly he appears fine. He wants people to believe he is the same old Cody. Inside, he's changed profoundly and those closest to him have seen that change. He has mood swings, he gets frustrated and it's not always easy to reason with him.

JT's compassionate personality was the perfect fit for Cody's anger and frustration. Cody was having a difficult time physically and emotionally; his inability to communicate well compounded the problem. JT wanted to make things easier for Cody. He wanted to see him reach his new potential, a potential they have yet to identify. JT helped him apply for benefits and tried to get him to understand he would never have gainful employment again. He explained he could do volunteer work and lecture in the hopes of helping other people, but police work was no longer an option. It wasn't easy for either of them.

Before the accident, everything Cody did revolved around police work; it was his life, his love, his future. And then it was gone. Some might have said Cody was cocky, others that he was sure of himself. When it came down to it, he was young and eager. He was kind and helpful when needed and a no nonsense stern cop when he pulled you over. He was living his dream, full of pride and wanting to do the best possible job.

When Cody heard that a state trooper was about to pull over two allegedly armed and dangerous suspects, he didn't want that trooper to be alone. He sped to the scene, as many officers do, when they respond to a call. The road conditions and traffic were not in his favor and he suffered a devastating crash. People have said he is lucky he didn't kill someone; what they don't realize is that he did kill someone. He killed the old Cody and a little bit of all of the people that loved him. They were all casualties that day. He takes full responsibility for his actions and the accident has humbled him. He has no ill will toward anyone.

It wasn't easy to get to that point. He's wondered why God left him on this earth. Why did he let him come back? What would that help if he blamed God or anyone else? It would actually hinder him from getting better.

But he was angry for a very long time; he lashed out at the people around him. Having his gun and badge taken away was the hardest part, but he says that as a Christian he has to be forgiving and non-judgmental. No one called 9-1-1 that day to intentionally injure Cody; a series of factors added up to create a life changing event and now he has to decide how to move on. He's still not sure what that means.

His feelings have ranged from sadness to anger and even suicidal thoughts. He's living in a world he doesn't recognize; he wants to be able to show emotion again and he knows how difficult it is for people to understand the person he is now.

"I'm in pain as we speak. I suffer mentally and physically every day but if I don't attempt to look at the positive in this world than it's not worth living. I can't do what God left me here to do if I am sitting around feeling sorry for myself. I'm not physically able to run. I have accepted that there are deficits that I will always have. It could be worse. There are officers that have it so much worse emotionally. Physically they may have gone through the same things but may not have had the emotional backing from the police and community. I have the best story. I was very loved, I still am. But the saddest part of my story is that my mom has cried for years.

"It's as real and raw as if it just happened yesterday."

Loving someone with a traumatic brain injury is difficult; the past is gone and the future is unknown. For a mother, it's devastating. Stephanie held vigil by Cody's bedside looking for the slightest hint that he was going to be okay — that he would live, that his brain would be intact.

When Cody was transferred from Memphis to Atlanta, Stephanie expected the doctors to tell her that the Memphis hospital was wrong and that Cody would fully recover. That he wouldn't have brain damage and life would be as it always had been. They didn't; they told her she was in denial and the Cody that survives will be very different than the Cody she knew. All she heard was that Cody would survive; she couldn't think about the rest yet.

Stephanie focused on getting Cody to respond in such a way that the doctors wouldn't tell her it was, "just a reflex". She wanted them to see he could hear her and was on his way back. On February 5, Stephanie's birthday, she begged him to give her a sign, and he did. He was able to hug her. For Stephanie, that was a turning point. The boy she loved and raised into a man would live. He would be able to move his limbs and understand what he was being told. Cody was back.

But he wasn't back, at least not the way he had been. The most difficult thing to understand was the man standing before her, nearly everything about him had changed – his laugh, looks, handwriting, personality, even his hair. What's even more difficult is the precarious world they live in. Although Stephanie loves and appreciates the new Cody, she sometimes misses the old Cody. But she is afraid to tell him, afraid for him to know the kind of pain she is in, or the effect the accident has had on her. She doesn't want him to feel unloved or abandoned; she doesn't want to give him one more thing to worry about.

Since the accident, Cody has had a few angry outbursts, some of which he doesn't remember. Through therapy, he's learned to control his behavior. What none of them can control is the fact he has no visible injuries so it is difficult for people to understand the internal injuries he does have. His medications, doctor's appointments and his inability to understand something as simple as what time it is, has left his family exhausted and alone.

Cody's father and brother try to reason with him; they don't understand Cody can't process things the way he used to. Physical exertion of any kind, including an hour on the phone, can leave him exhausted for days. The amount of concentration and effort needed to perform simple tasks is monumental. Many things need to be done for him and those tasks fall onto Stephanie.

She makes sure his expired food is thrown out, his medications are being taken and his doctors keep watch. She also has to manage the lawyers and the insurance companies, fighting for benefits as simple as eye glasses, something he now needed because of an eye injury. Workers compensation abandoned Cody as it has abandoned so many officers like him. The more time Stephanie spent fighting for Cody, the more she risked her own job. There's no local support for families like hers and she doesn't know where to turn. She relies on research and will power to get through the day.

Stephanie lives for small glimpses of normalcy. Although she gets panic attacks riding in a car with Cody, one of her sweetest memories since the accident was in a car. Cody began to sing and Stephanie recognized his old voice. His words were well-pronounced and she couldn't speak; she simply wanted him to sing forever so they could both feel like everything was okay. It was a bittersweet reminder of their lives before the accident. Lives that were filled with friends and normalcy.

"I want people to know how this has changed our life," Stephanie explains. "I need to talk but it's so hard, it is very emotional. People think I should just be thankful he is alive and don't understand how different our life is now. That's very upsetting for me. I am thankful, but the brain injury doesn't go away; it will be here for the rest of our lives and people don't understand that. I had never been around anyone who has dealt with this either but it changes you, how you deal with the injured person and your own life. Not only did he lose friends, so did we."

Cody's injury has taken a physical and emotional toll on everyone; the biggest hurdle is finding the proper care and making sure insurance will cover it. Stephanie has no experience caring for someone with a catastrophic injury and there is no help readily available. Police departments and their unions are not equipped to handle the aftermath. Stephanie's wish is that anyone serving the public be taken care of, that facilities be provided to assist them. Instead, each family starts their journey surrounded by overwhelming well-wishers and fundraisers, but they end up alone hoping to find the right resource and support to get them through. It's a long, arduous task that no family is ever prepared for.

Some families have compared their needs to those of soldiers returning from battle and long for a resource like the Veterans Administration that provide long-term support and care for injured soldiers, Stephanie's family is no different. She spends hours reading and researching trying to find out how Cody's medications are affecting him, what his future will be like, and what her next battle will be for benefits to keep Cody going.

Cody was lucky in one respect, his community and the police department threw their support behind him immediately after the accident. He loves to talk about the thousands of cards and letters of support he received from around the country. The pride in his voice is both heartwarming and saddening; he loved his career, he loved the support of his "brothers and sisters" but he will become a memory like many other disabled officers and the cards will eventually stop.

Right now, he's focusing more on his physical pain rather than what will happen in the future. Physical therapy is still a struggle because he is in constant pain. The implant that sends signals through the spinal cord to the brain to try to trick him into thinking he has no pain doesn't always work. His psychological care is just as challenging. Cody has gone from being self-assured to a self-conscious, lonely man who tries to mask his real pain with hopeful words and subtle requests for affirmation. He is living in a world no one should have to.

"I've become more secluded because of my speech deficit. I am very self-conscious about my speech and how I come across to girls. I'm not as sharp as I used to be and my personal relationships have suffered. I believe that God did this for a reason and there is a plan. I don't know what it is right now but I do believe there is a plan. Maybe I will be able to save one other person from making the same mistakes."

Some days he comes to terms with himself, other days he thinks about what could have been. What if Chris Wamble hadn't called 9-1-1 that day? What if he hadn't been speeding? What if the car hadn't pulled back into the road? What if he wasn't so eager to help? Cody asks himself those questions daily. While his mother is trying to protect Cody from her feelings, he is trying to protect her from his. What's ironic is that they both miss the same things; they both miss their lives and who Cody was before the accident. Perhaps they can find a way to share their pain with each other in such a way it helps them heal. If they do, they can find a way to love the life they have and the people they have both become. Maybe then they can find some peace.

Until then, Stephanie will continue to worry, cry and struggle to get her family through each day. Cody will wistfully think of the police department and will miss the dream he once held in his hand.

Part Six

OFFICER SUICIDE

It's not up to you how you fall. It's up to you how far you let yourself fall and how long it takes you to get back up and stand on your own two feet.

- Sir Tac Jeffrey Mitchell

Not all threats to an officer's life come from other people. Sometimes the worst enemy can be internal. The police suicide rate is something of a debate among academics because of misclassification of cause of death due to the embarrassment or shame it may cause the family or the law enforcement agency. Comparisons with the general population's suicide rate are not representative of the average law enforcement officer. Therefore trying to determine if the law enforcement rate is higher or lower than the general public is impossible. It is believed the suicide rate for a law enforcement officer lies somewhere between 16 and 18 per 100,000 officers (Clark, 2012). To put this estimate in perspective, 133 line of duty deaths were documented in 2012 which includes all accidental, felonious assault, and motor vehicle fatalities. A study from the same year (O'Hara, Violanti, Levenson Jr., & Clark Sr., 2012) reports 126 officers died from their own hand. An officer is almost just as likely to be killed in the line of duty as they are to kill themselves.

While the estimated suicide rate is disconcerting in itself, if we consider most officers have been through psychological screening as part of the vetting process before they were offered a job, the numbers become more disconcerting. If the officer had a clean bill of mental health prior to joining the law enforcement agency, we must consider what changes in these officers through their career and try to determine how to reduce or prevent law enforcement suicide. As was discussed, high pressure, violence, and resistance to seeking help from sources outside the law enforcement guild are ever present throughout a career. Each of these factors in and of itself could probably increase the chances of police suicide. Coupled with a single traumatic event or cumulative stress of multiple incidents and an officer may become overwhelmed. Even if an officer does not have the immediate onset of a post-traumatic stress disorder or other psychological damage from a critical incident, they may be masking their emotions. This covering will likely lead to long-term issues which could be addressed and corrected if officers were provided assistance early on (Kates, 1999). Early interventions would likely reduce officer suicides, even if these interventions were mandated by department policy. Agencies who adopt policies that address the psychological welfare of their officers through peer support, critical

incident debriefings, professional counseling services, or the use of chaplain services are likely to
benefit fiscally and through improvement in agency
morale.

DON

Seven weeks on the job as a rookie found Don ducking for cover. He heard cracks and booms which he knew to be gunshots and instinctively hid. "What are you doing?" his Field Training Officer (FTO) exclaimed.

"They're shooting at us!"

"Shots are fired every night; get used to it."

Don found himself in a city where he would frequently see muzzle flashes and know that many of those bullets were directed at him. Eventually, he would find himself sitting on his couch playing Russian roulette with his own gun directing bullets at himself.

Growing up in a small town, the first one in his family to graduate college, Don hadn't always set his sights on policing; he planned to be an attorney. After hearing an officer lecture in one of his courses, his interest was piqued and Don began to consider this occupation. An off the cuff bet from another officer while eating Taco Bell and watching COPS set Don on a path that would eventually destroy him. The Los Angeles Police Department was hiring and his friend bet Don wouldn't apply. Don picked up his touch-tone phone, called information to get the phone number for the LAPD and requested an application.

Don didn't make the cut for the LAPD and he admits that after the Rodney King incident, he was glad he didn't. However, he wasn't swayed from police work. He put himself through the law enforcement academy, bettered himself physically and landed a job with another large city less than a year later.

At the age of 24, a white guy from a town of 7,000 people he began his job as a police officer in a large, diverse city which rarely slept. Don thought police work would give him the opportunity to help people in a way he could not as a lawyer. He was naïve and unprepared for what he would experience.

Being assigned to the "hood," surrounded by gangs daily, getting shot at and hearing a man say to his child, "You see them mother fucking po-po's? You hate them. You hate them," shocked Don. He wondered why people hated him so much; what had he done to garner such contempt? Happily married, not wanting to bring the job home, Don took to drinking after work. It started innocently enough; a few beers with the guys to unwind, a way to stop feeling the effects of their shifts. Just enough to numb their minds, not enough to appear hung over for their next shift. Just enough.

While Don was on duty, there was nothing to protect his mind. Helicopters flew overhead while he chased down gang members. The police watched as thugs shot at each other, dropped weapons and magazines and ran. They tended to the wounded asking, "Who shot you?" The reply, "Fuck you." They'd call the gang unit and if the victim died, he died. It was over, that's it. No one would offer information; there were no witnesses and therefore no case. There was effectively no crime to solve, that's the way the streets wanted it to be.

By the time he was 37, Don was a watch commander listening to a young officer ask if he was going to be alright. Dispatched to a call of shots fired, the suspect hid behind a dumpster and as soon as the police cruiser rolled up, he appeared and began shooting. The suspect then jumped onto the hood of the patrol car and shot through the windshield. The officer was shot through the shoulder and the groin, his best friend in the cruiser behind him watching the scene unfold.

The suspect had been hit by the second car and was in custody; he would live. Don began cutting the clothes off the injured officer, not know if he was going to live but assuring him he would while simultaneously trying to calm the man's best friend.

"I just thought, 'Holy fuck, this shit is too real.' I didn't know if he was going to make it because of all the blood. I'm thinking, I have kids, what if this were me? What the hell am I doing here?"

Gunfire wasn't the only thing that affected Don. "Now I am seeing dead people, dead babies, and trying to put people back together on the street. I can't get them in body bags because they are in pieces. I'm at a four-way intersection at the scene of a bad accident and I'm trying to figure out what to do with the severed arm of a dead woman so we can get traffic moving again.

"I began to lose sight of who we were and why we were involved in these types of life and death situations. People are constantly dying around me and I can't control it. As police officers we are taught to be in control of a situation and as people die we aren't. You have 30 people at a pool party and someone turned their back for a moment and now I am trying to save a 2-year-old. It didn't make sense to me anymore. I was losing my sense of reality and why these things continued to happen. I began to lose hope and faith which is absolutely necessary in life. I chose alcohol to deal with it."

Don had PTSD for years and didn't know it; he wanted to control the things that were happening around him and he couldn't. He didn't feel he could talk openly about what he witnessed at work and felt there were very few people who could listen. When he tried to talk to his family, it became too difficult for them to hear. He didn't want to hurt them so he began to suppress his feelings and his experiences.

On the outside, things looked normal. Don had a successful career; he moved quickly through the ranks, obtained extra training on his own time and received multiple awards and accolades. "I was the superstar of the month. I never had a complaint. I was an FTO, a detective and worked hard to be successful in my career. My wife understood my desire to be successful and the importance of that success to my psyche."

As his career progressed, so did his drinking. It was now more than a drink to numb his mind. He was an alcoholic. Don realized he needed to stop; he needed to find another outlet before it got him into trouble. He stopped drinking but failed to find another outlet. This would prove to be a near fatal mistake. Don struggled under the weight of his inability to protect the public and to suppress the harsh images that scorched his mind. Politics pushed him over the edge.

"In some departments, there is a double standard. You are doing your best to just do your job and follow the policies, and someone violates them. Some people within the department are held to higher standards than others; some are forgiven more quickly. This will break you down. Wondering what standard you will be held to and how you will be treated becomes stressful. When you see others are treated differently based on relationships or favors, the organizational stress becomes more stressful than what is taking place on the streets. If you violate accidentally or on purpose and are treated more harshly because you don't have a connection it creates an organizational culture that is detrimental to the entire department."

The more Don moved up in his department, the more aware he became of what some would call small favors and others would call corruption. Don preferred the latter and he sought to put an end to it. It had been going on for so long, he was met with great resistance. Resistance that smeared his name and forced him into early retirement.

Without his job or alcohol, Don became suicidal. He rode through the ranks with a clean jacket, thought he did everything right and now he was set adrift without his job. A job that was his identity.

"I'm an officer in my mind. I always will be. I was a highly decorated officer. I was respected, oversaw 6 substations and over a million people each night. I still talk and drive like an officer. My family doesn't understand me, they don't understand what I've been through, and they don't understand what it meant to me. My identity? It's gone because I challenged what I saw as corruption; I wanted a better department."

Don left police work for good 4 years ago. He continues to be a highly functioning, successful person. He and his family have had their ups and downs between jobs, but he's found himself in a new career helping the public in a field parallel to law enforcement but the scars haven't healed. After 5 years of sobriety, Don began peer counseling; he wanted to help other officers in their time of need. Listening to their stories, hearing their voices sent him into a tailspin and he began drinking again. His good intentions proved to be the end of his marriage.

Things at home began to spiral out of control because of his return to the bottle; his wife of nineteen years had enough and wanted a divorce. Don currently sleeps only 2-3 hours per night and relives every negative memory from his years as a police officer. He has little control over where his mind goes and has become frustrated, agitated and a danger to himself. He has sat with a gun to his head three times. He has lived because fate has decided it's not his time and sheer willpower. He knows his children need him; he knows he has to find a way to survive and to heal.

While his family surrounds him at meal time, he struggles with finding a way to die. "But then what? They find me dead and that's it. What then? What happens to my family? It's a bitter battle I fight every day. I'm trying not to drink, trying to find a way out and it's hard. My whole life was my career. A career that damaged me, but I was committed to it. I wanted it. The same career that was taken from me because I wanted every other cop to walk the straight and narrow, to give us all a good name. Hypocrisy, prosecuting people for something they do themselves.

"I lost who I was a long time ago. My purpose in life ended. I want to die but I know I can't. I want the demons to stop haunting me. Now it's time to check myself in for help. I go in Monday for thirty days of treatment. I am dying. My heart is going to give out or I am going to kill myself. I need to find my way back and it's time."

Two days from this writing, Don will check into a treatment center for in-depth psychological counseling. With the help of a national group aiding first responders, he's found a safe place with the resources to help people with his type of trauma. Don knows how urgent his situation has become and not only because of the number of times he had a gun to his head. Other officers from his former department have committed suicide over the last few years, one taking his wife and children with him. Many people have called those officers weak or evil; they have said their deaths have effectively erased all of the good they have done over the course of their careers. What those people don't realize is they aren't evil. They have been affected by evil and sometimes, evil has a way of taking you with it. They weren't evil; they were overcome by it.

MARCI

Be a good little girl. Do your job. Don't cry. Don't complain. Just do it. For twenty years, that's how Marci lived. No one came right out and said it; they didn't have to. At age 24, Marci started her law enforcement career as a reserve officer. An injury at the shooting range nearly brought Marci to tears, and she endured ridicule at the hands of her peers. "Don't you dare cry!" yelled her supervisor. At that moment Marci learned to hide her emotions to avoid being seen as weak. She knew going into law enforcement was not going to be easy and being a female was always going to work against her, so she vowed to be as good as, or better than, the men alongside her and to never show weakness. Twenty years of strength, or so she thought. Marci believed she was protecting herself, helping herself, when in fact she was slowly destroying herself.

Being a police officer is hard enough, but being a female officer is often harder. Many of them struggle to find their place in a physically and emotionally demanding environment but they are there because, like Marci, they love the job. Marci loved it enough to put herself through the academy; she had no connections in law enforcement and earned her place one small step at a time. As the only female patrol officer in a small department, Marci learned as much as she could and started polishing her reputation. She wanted bigger and better things.

Four years later, in 1998, she quickly found that bigger wasn't necessarily better. She transferred to a larger city and police force at a time when ecstasy was becoming popular and raves were becoming more frequent. Called to the scene of an attempted carjacking at a local rave concert, Marci found a woman who had been punched in the face multiple times. Armed with a description of the suspect, she quickly found him walking down the street less than a mile from the scene. Marci immediately exited her vehicle and ordered the suspect to stop. She notified dispatch she was out with a possible suspect.

Rather than running from the police, as suspects are known to do, the suspect jumped onto the hood of Marci's patrol car and just stared at her. Knowing that behavior like his was an indication something was terribly wrong, Marci's training kicked in. She knew she was all alone. It was a busy night and her backup was miles away. With her weapon drawn, Marci ordered the suspect onto the ground. He complied and sank to his knees in front of the police vehicle. Placing his elbows on the front push bar, he then placed his hands in a praying position. Marci knew the situation was still volatile despite his compliance; she ordered him face down on the ground into "prone position." Marci stood approximately 20 feet away, gun drawn and expedited her backup over the police radio.

At first, he complied and laid face down on the ground. Almost instantly, he changed his position, jumped up and ran toward Marci yelling, "Fuck you bitch." Before she knew it, he had one hand locked on her gun hand, attempting to take her weapon. The suspect began punching her in the head with his fist, several times.

Punch after punch, Marci began to get light-headed. It was that final blow to her temple that made her realize she was fighting for her life. As she was about to black out she knew she only had one option. She repositioned her right leg back in an effort to give her a stronger stance and more balance. She squeezed the trigger of her gun, which was still being controlled by the suspect.

She fired one round. The suspect fell to the ground immediately with what she thought was a bullet to his stomach. Marci then did what seemed natural. Seeing the suspect was no longer a threat, she holstered her weapon and notified dispatch shots had been fired and the suspect was down. The suspect was making gurgling sounds but appeared to still be alive. Marci began to comfort the suspect telling him to breathe and that an ambulance was on its way. As patrol cars arrived on scene, along with the shift sergeant, Marci was verbally comforting the man who had just tried to take her life. Per protocol, Marci was immediately taken from the scene and driven to the police station to be interviewed. By the time she reached the station for her debriefing, she had been told the man she had shot had died on scene by a bullet to his heart. An overwhelming feeling of remorse engulfed Marci, even though she knew she would be the one lying dead had she not shot him. They would later find out that he had PCP, marijuana, alcohol, and ecstasy in his system and was court marshaled from the Marines for domestic violence.

It was a good shoot and there were no internal reviews, but there was jealousy and second-guessing amongst her peers. Marci learned the hard way this was common behavior between officers. Trying to deal with her own emotions and the realization police work was unpredictable, Marci still pulled herself together and accepted what had happened.

Despite her obvious injuries, some officers questioned Marci's version of events. They thought she had tripped and accidentally shot the suspect or became scared because he came at her. Even though Marci had support from administration, her family and friends, it was the lack of confidence and the Monday morning quarterbacking from her peers that bothered her. She would be asked questions like, "How much bigger was he than you?" or "Why couldn't you just use your baton?" These questions and judgments were from officers that had never been close to being involved in a shooting, yet they were the first to judge another officer's actions. Others became jealous: "I can't believe you were in a shooting before me!" Others looked upon her with awe and respect knowing Marci was fully capable of "pulling the trigger" when needed. Marci simply wished it hadn't happened, but she never second-guessed herself. She didn't want to live with the fact she had killed a man. Over the years it would eat away at her and become yet another invisible injury she would have to contend with.

Marci continued her career as a law enforcement officer without incident. She was selected to be one of two officers to join the department's newest juvenile program involving one police officer and one probation officer. Just prior to starting her new assignment, Marci had gotten married to a man she had met while on duty. He was a paramedic and they met at the local hospital, in the hallway. This was the first time Marci had ever been romantically involved with another first responder.

Even though her husband was a paramedic and saw horrific scenes as well, Marci would come home from work and not talk about her job. Marci did a good job separating her professional life from her personal life. In 2003 Marci gave birth to her one and only daughter, Kali. Marci was thrilled to become a mom but knew she still had to dedicate her life to her career while juggling parenthood. Marci had a saying that she lived by to help make it easier for her to live her personal life normally, "I am my husband's wife and my daughter's mother."

While Marci was pregnant she was placed on light duty which meant working the front desk. She got involved in her department's Crisis Intervention Training and became one of the department's coordinators. This entailed assisting in the department's in-house training, and networking with other county agencies such as the Department of Behavioral Health (DBH), the judicial system, and nonprofit organizations. She attended county mental health meetings, became the law enforcement representative for crisis intervention with the police academy, and was her department's liaison between law enforcement and DBH. Over the course of 10 years, Marci continued her education in mental health and accumulated over 160 hours of specialized training.

In 2005, leveraging her history of mental health and crisis intervention, she became the first Homeless Advocate Officer for her department and county. Marci earned recognition and awards by linking the homeless in her city with services and organizations in the area. She also launched a program which taught the mentally ill how to handle their interactions with the police to ensure positive outcomes.

If Marci simply had to work with the homeless in her city, things may have ended differently for her, but she did her due time working the streets, which she loved to do. As a patrol officer she witnessed gruesome scenes and was directly involved in handling numerous traumatic incidents, such as being on scene while an officer was shot, being shot at during a police riot, dead newborn babies she held in her arms, removing a toddler from a pool after it had drowned, seeing a corpse's throat slit from ear to ear, and suicides by hangings, overdoses, and gunshot wounds to the head. Years of direct and secondary trauma take a toll on one's psyche. Worst of all, the killing of another human being manages to manifest itself in one's memory, despite what she tells herself. "How confident you are in your job and that you can live with your actions is what will really carry you through. I didn't have nightmares or second guess the decision I made that morning of my shooting. I was able to detach myself by not getting too close. I never read the report nor did I wish to know his name. The less I knew, the better off I was not letting it affect me. That's how I was able to handle it."

By 2009, Marci had earned fourteen awards and recognitions including the 2005 Woman of Achievement, nomination as Officer of the Year, and one of the Top Ten People Who Made a Difference in her city. She is especially proud of this recognition because she was nominated by a thirteen year old girl she helped through probation and off the street. All of this came with a price: her marriage. Marci knows her devotion to her job, especially the homeless program, was one of the main causes that led to her divorce. She was always the first in and last out, never took sick time, worked hard and even harder when she was injured.

In addition to piling up the recognition, Marci also piled up injuries. Over the course of her career she had sustained neck and back injuries, cervical spine injuries, broken fingers, knee injuries and a shoulder injury. The list goes on. She didn't take time off of work, nor did she make a fuss; it was all part of the job.

Marci documented her first injury in 2000: a herniated disc in her lower back. She never took time off work for that injury until 2009 when her disc had torn. She refused to have surgery and chose to live a healthier life. She lost 65 pounds over the course of a year and felt stronger than ever. The lower back is one of the most common areas of all police injuries. Officers suffer cumulative back injuries from jumping, lifting, the weight of duty belts, and other demands put on their bodies.

Marci also had a problem with her Kevlar vest; it no longer fit her properly due to the weight loss. She routinely stopped to tighten the straps that bore down on her shoulders and rib cage because it would work its way loose throughout the course of her shift. This motion aggravated her previous neck injuries. In April 2012, she developed muscle spasms to the left side of her neck and collar bone so severe she couldn't move her head to one side. She experienced severe headaches that would last for days. Marci did what she was supposed to do: she continued to work full duty while she went to physical therapy. She even went as far as getting a prescription for a custom fit vest which was approved by workers compensation. Unfortunately, in an effort to save the city some money, the civilian responsible for ordering the vests ordered her a standard vest, just like everyone else. Marci's neck continued to ache and her injuries worsened.

Determined not to let injury affect her performance or her reputation, she continued on and would earn five more honors between 2010 and 2013, including the Woman of the Year presented by the State Senate during Woman's History Month, and a Lifesaving Award for saving the life of a quadriplegic in a house fire.

Her devotion to her job, at the expense of her own physical well-being, now caught up to her. In September 2012, she damaged her left shoulder in a fight with a suspect. It couldn't have happened at a worse time: her department was in the midst of filing bankruptcy. Officers were leaving to other police departments, people were calling in sick or using their vacation. There were only seven officers on shift where there were formerly 15, equipment was breaking down, and the administration sent them back on the road daily telling them they had nothing to worry about. Administration tried to convince officers things would get better, knowing things were just getting worse. Marci felt as if she was one of those wind-up toy soldiers and was told to just march out of briefing and go work her shift as if nothing were wrong and take on the work load with her shift being half staffed.

Having spent eighteen years convincing herself she needed to work harder as a female officer to succeed, to get respect, and to be taken seriously by her peers, Marci continued as though she were fine and needed to hide her pain and emotions. Because her injury was getting worse, she began taking Vicodin to get through the day and be able to manage the pain that was continually increasing. She was also trying to understand why the city was allowing the department to fall apart, why they were being told to "just get out there and remain professional," and why the declining morale was being ignored. It was very hard to remain professional when community members were yelling profanities out their car windows at officers as they would perform a traffic stop or respond to a call. By November, Marci was unable to hide her emotional distress any longer. Officers were told prior to hitting the streets they have to remember who their tax payers are and to continue to remain professional at all cost due to media filming officers actions daily. All because city officials had placed blame on public safety for the city's financial woes. Marci made a comment out loud that caused her sergeant to ask her if she was fit for duty. She was unable to look him in the eye or give an answer.

She tried to be the good little girl she was always expected to be and was fighting back the emotions. He asked again, "Are you fit for duty?" Marci couldn't lie nor hold it in any longer. She finally broke down and started to cry. She had been overwhelmed with stress from working while injured, her fellow officer's safety was being jeopardized daily, she was over worked due to minimal staffing, and her ex-husband was threatening to take her to court for child and spousal support. Out of concern for her mental well-being, she was ordered off the street and told to go speak with someone at their employee assistance program.

She spent almost three months on psychiatric leave disguised as sick leave. The stigma of having psychological problems was so great she had denied a claim to be written up and had taken her time off as "sick time." Administration was supportive and allowed her the time off because of her stellar career and dedication to the department. Marci spent that time working on her mental state. She was unable to admit to her injuries for fear of being labeled or mistreated as a lazy officer or someone who just wants to get off the streets and retire. Marci willingly came back to work to avoid marring her reputation. She refused to admit she had PTSD or reveal the extent of her injuries. Even though she had been diagnosed years prior with anxiety, insomnia and for having an obsessive compulsive personality, no officer wants to be labeled with mental illness or have it on their permanent record for that matter.

Only six months after coming back to the streets, Marci responded to a residential burglary call. As she apprehended a suspect she experienced electric shock running up both her wrists. As an automatic reaction she let go due to the shock radiating up her wrists. The suspect had to be apprehended by Marci's beat partner. Guilt and disappointment set in and she felt as if she had let her partner down by her lack of performance. After that particular call, her sergeant pulled her aside and asked why she did not help her partner in apprehending the suspect. The sergeant didn't see when Marci went to grab for the suspect, she only saw Marci standing there after her partner apprehended the suspect after Marci let go. Marci danced around the truth to avoid being forced off the streets due to her injuries so she merely told her sergeant she was unable to assist with the apprehension due to her bad positioning in the doorway. She had just told a white lie and did not want to reveal her true pain.

June 10, 2013 is a date embedded in Marci's mind forever. That was the day she worked her last shift on patrol. She didn't know it would be the very last day she would ever wear her badge and police uniform again. Marci made the decision to request to be taken off the streets due to the severity of her injuries. In her eagerness to return to work, Marci knew she had finally become an officer safety issue for herself and for her peers. Voluntarily going to light duty was frowned upon in her department, because without an obvious physical injury she was categorized as someone who was faking, or taking advantage of the system. Marci was assigned to work the front desk where she was to handle phone reports and all law enforcement crime reports that walked into the station. Even though Marci appeared okay on the outside, her morale continued to plummet over the glares and snide remarks she got. The sergeant who pulled her aside had told the patrol captain that Marci put herself on light duty because she was yelled at for not helping her beat partner take a suspect into custody. Hearing that rumor was devastating to Marci. Knowing the truth behind why she took herself off the streets, it bothered her that her superior came to an assumption as to why Marci was on light duty.

Eventually, Marci's cervical spine, neck and shoulder injury would put her in the emergency room just weeks after being put on light duty. She tried to come back to work, but on July 24, 2013 she was taken off light duty and placed on medical leave for the first time in her career. A year later she was deemed disabled and was forced to retire.

Marci had spent her career accepting impact after impact to her body; she believed – rightly or wrongly – that she had no other choice. She knew she was to blame; she knew she didn't take care of herself well enough. But she also believed the consequences could have been worse. "I had to weigh out what it would do to my career as a female cop. Did I want people talking about me the same way I hear them talking about other female officers who claim injuries? I worked with a female officer who was rear ended at only 10mph and retired on a disability on a neck injury. I wasn't going to be categorized as she was. I chose to be a good little girl and go back to work.

"June 10, 2013 was the last day I wore my badge. I knew I had become a hazard and had to get off the street. Something no officer ever thought they would have to do on their own. My peers and the people of the city deserved more than what I could give them at that point."

Marci began to experience what many injured officers do: the long fight with the city insurance company to get treatment and the engagement of attorneys to help them get what they need and deserve.

Home, injured, in and out of the emergency room, doctors were trying to pinpoint her medical issues. It took nearly three months before her workers compensation adjuster made contact with her and approved treatment; treatment long overdue. Ignoring her injuries for so long had only added to the problems. She had a slight bulged disc in her cervical spine with a compressed nerve root, which caused a numbing and tingling sensation in both arms and weakness in both hands. Her left shoulder pain was more than just a tear in her rotator cup; it was later found she also had thoracic outlet syndrome in her left shoulder which caused her to lose circulation in her left arm when raised above her shoulder. The pain she endured over the three months without treatment was indescribable. The only thing that kept her sane was the pain medication her doctor prescribed to her. She had tested positive for an autoimmune disease and had developed neuropathy in her legs. At this point she had no idea what was happening to her body; she felt as if it was shutting down. She had finally reached a point where she couldn't walk or drive and had to call an ambulance to drive her the quarter mile to the hospital for the fourth time. This was her breaking point.

As with most departments, once an officer is off work on an injury, they are left to manage their crisis alone. No one from the department called Marci to check on her other than one female officer, a captain, that she had been best friends with for over 12 years. Other administrators didn't bother to call knowing that her friend had been in communication with her.

"It's not the same thing having a longtime friend call me to check on me verses my immediate supervisors or patrol captain calling to check on me. All I wanted was to feel like I mattered."

Marci, like thousands of other injured officers, became a part of the forgotten population. She was shunned from her entire department just because she took time off for her injuries at a time the department and city was in a crisis.

On April 4, 2014, Marci was told what every officer never wants to hear. "You're done. You will never do patrol work again. Your injuries are too severe to work the streets."

"I felt as if my heart was ripped out of my chest. My whole life was gone, my career, everything I worked so hard for, all gone. No one called. No one came by. It's like I had never been a cop. That hurt most of all. I would have taken a bullet for my beat partners and now I no longer exist. I know I should have asked for help sooner, but I couldn't. There are certain types that have a really hard time asking for help; I'm one of them."

Marci had barely been holding things together, and only for the sake of her daughter. The weeks her daughter stayed with her she put on her brave face and functioned as though nothing was wrong. When her daughter went to spend the week with her father, Marci laid in bed in a deep depression. She felt alone. Her department had a peer support group but no one from the group had called to check on her. She was even a peer support member for her department and had called one of the officers that was home injured from a gunshot wound to his leg while she herself was home injured. That officer was being checked on daily, from peers, administration, officers from other departments. "Departments should not pick and choose who they call and check on. A gunshot wound should not be more important than another type of injury. All officers with an injury matter. What happened to the Thin Blue Line family everyone always claims to be?" She committed twenty years of her life to a career and a city that she loved and they abandoned her in her time of need. An officer prematurely retired because of injury is quickly forgotten.

She became addicted to pain meds and began drinking to ease the physical and emotional pain. Her sister took away her guns and she dwelled on her lost life. The very thing that she allowed to define her was gone.

"My identity was gone. Who am I now? What can I do? They took my passion. They stole my career away from me. I wasn't ready to retire. We risk our lives for what? To be ignored by our own peers and to be treated as a nobody by workers comp, by doctors, and even by my attorney? They only care about themselves and what's in it for them?"

Marci fell into a deep, dark hole and didn't know how she got there. One night, while her daughter was with her father, Marci took what could have been a deadly mix of pills and alcohol. She texted her sister, Donna, whom she is very close to as she was dozing off. Her texts were not making any sense. Marci was texting things like, "Please forgive me," "If anything should happen to me," and "I'm sorry I failed." Living less than a mile away, her sister came right over and found Marci lying in bed nearly unconscious. Her sister rushed her to the hospital where she was treated for an overdose.

"When the fog began to clear, I realized I had to push through for my daughter. All the complaining about not getting checked on didn't matter anymore. My badge didn't define me; I defined the badge. I decided I needed to start paying it forward by telling my story. I was kept alive for a reason. There are so many officers going through the same thing; not knowing who they can turn to, hiding behind their pain, caving to peer pressure or not even aware they have PTSD. I want to help them. I get it."

It was an uphill climb. She didn't fully understand why she tried to kill herself and has very little memory about all that truly happened the night she tried to take her own life. She knew she had to be strong for her daughter and that she had to try to make her family understand.

"Families don't get it. We have to hide our feelings; men have to hide it more. My mother thought I took the pills accidentally. She told me to get a pill box and be more careful. She also has told me she knows how I feel, about my pain and being retired. No, she doesn't. You can't compare it. It's not the same."

In January 2013, Marci began her life journey to help other officers and their families understand what it takes to support a first responder. She became a crisis call taker for Safe Call Now.

"Whether its depression, PTSD, or chemical dependency, Safe Call Now can help. Safe Call Now helped me and now I want to thank them by helping save the lives of other first responders."

Marci wants acknowledgement that there are very few trained professionals who can handle the type of trauma officers are dealing with and that their family members also need to understand how to help an officer in crisis. More importantly, departments need to understand and support their officers in their time of need, no matter what the injury is.

A year into Marci's retirement, she still hasn't been treated properly; she needs surgery which requires a rib to be removed, and her attorney and her doctor have downplayed its urgency. She took matters into her own hands and dismissed her attorney and replaced her current primary treating physician with a doctor she picked, not one that an attorney or workers comp adjuster picked for her. "I am taking control of my life. I will not allow others to benefit from my misfortune any longer. My life matters."

Other than being a Peer Support Specialist for Safe Call Now, Marci started several different programs that help offer support to other first responders. She has created a Suicide Prevention for

First Responders Campaign that is affiliated with Safe Call Now, she started a support group for female law enforcement officers across the nation, and she fulfilled one of her dreams by starting her very own non-profit organization called, "Sisters of the Shield Foundation." Marci has a lot to be proud of. "I have learned to wear my tragedies as armor, not as shackles."

She knows the importance of peer support. However, neither her volunteer work nor her medical pension pays all the bills. She recently sold her house of fifteen years, a 112 year old home with a yard and a pool. Previously making a comfortable living, she now lives at poverty level. She worked her entire adult life, paying her own way and now she has to ask for government help for her and her daughter's medical insurance. "It took every ounce of courage to walk into the county office to apply for medical so that my daughter and I would be medically insured. I had to set my pride aside and accept the fact that my entire lifestyle had to change. Besides having to give up our home I had to sacrifice my wants such as nails and only live with needs.

"I feel like I keep losing. I lost my job, my house, my identity, my income, and a lot of my friends. Where do I turn? Who helps the helper? In my case, who helps the crisis call taker? Secondary trauma is just as serious as primary trauma.

"It's confusing because despite what I've lost, I know God shut a door and opened another one. I truly believe I am here to help save lives. I have since dedicated my life to help reduce police suicide. It is so rewarding when another first responder says

'Thanks, you made me feel a lot better,' when it took all the courage they got to pick up the phone in the first place. That's what keeps me going. I don't ever want to give that up.

"I knew what I was getting myself into when I became a police officer. I knew I was signing up for a life filled with stress, looking evil right in the eye, and witnessing horrific scenes that can never be unseen. I knew what I was going into. What I didn't know was what would happen after I got out."

Part Seven

RESILIENCE

If you're going through hell, keep going.
- Winston Churchill

Not all officers who have faced a psychological injury are going to have long-term consequences, and even two officers facing the same incident may not respond in the same manner (Artwohl & Christensen, 1997). Some officers may be able to recover better than others because they are more resilient. Resilience is the individual's ability to recover following a stressful event. There is a noted difference in protective factors between resilient officers and non-resilient officers following a critical incident (Prati & Pietrantoni, 2010). Determination of resilience in a study of Italian police officers helped identify some of these risks and protective features found in officers. Socially supportive structures such as family, friend, and peer support play a significant role in resilience. The individual officers' self-esteem levels were determined to affect the ability to recover from a traumatic event. One of the more interesting findings in the study was length of service affected the level of resilience, with officers who had the longest length of service at the time of the traumatic incident not faring as well as those with shorter lengths of service. This discovery is likely a result of the cumulative effect of stress from a career filled with multiple exposures to critical incidents and the associated trauma which had not been resolved (Prati & Pietrantoni, 2010). A study in 1997 found that introversion, mental or emotional exhaustion at the time of the trauma, and insufficient recovery time post incident are all linked to the increased onset of post-traumatic stress disorder (Carlier, Lamberts, & Gersons, 1997). Some of these risk factors and preventative measures can be addressed by agency policy while others are up to the individual to control.

Most officers and people in general, will be able to cope over the long run with chronic or critical incident stress without any significant impairment (Kates, 1999), but if there will be long-term effects, then early intervention must be done to increase the chance of a successful outcome. In addition, early intervention shortens the total recovery time necessary for the officer.

Another method utilized to increase resilience is pre-incident training and education. Resiliency is variable in each individual and is affected by the individual's past coping ability, genetics, and established support systems. Law enforcement officers who know what could happen to their body and mind following a critical incident can adjust more quickly and recognize the symptoms for what they are, rather than deal with any anxiety associated with their sudden onset (Grossman & Christensen,

2008). Anxiety, loss of sleep, flashbacks, and memory loss are all common among officers involved in a traumatic event. Officers need to understand their reactions are normal responses to unusual events and there is not something wrong with them, and this needs to be made clear from the first stage of intervention and continue through professional psychological care. Officers should be briefed on how the mind works after a traumatic occurrence so they can better cope with the flood of post incident emotions, memory gaps, anger, and family member responses (Artwohl & Christensen, 1997). Not knowing the effects of trauma on the mind only increases the severity of these problems, specifically anxiety levels.

One of the last layers of resilience is the result of physical fitness. Fitness can assist with not only physical survival, but mental survival following a traumatic incident. There is extensive evidence to show physical fitness can assist with controlling anxiety and depression as well as increased resistance to the harmful effects of stress (Taylor, et al., 2008). Physical fitness helps the body deal with the cataclysm of chemicals dumped into the body during life or death events.

MAGGIE

People are born emotionally intact; as they grow, holes are poked in their beliefs, souls, and emotions. Eventually, we all resemble sieves, filtering out the bad, trying to hold on to the good. Maggie is like that, except that as a police officer the holes are a little larger because the things she needs to filter out are much bigger. Unfortunately, not everything bad escapes and she's left with too much to process on a daily basis.

Trying to explain this to rookies has been difficult. They often say, "I hope this job doesn't change me." What they don't yet know is it is inevitable: you will change, somehow, and it's out of your control. It's not something they immediately understand; it needs to be experienced. They will develop a new sieve, one specially reserved for first responders; every officer will have a filter that doesn't work quite right, and it will cause them to have a hard time letting go of certain things. For Maggie, the "child filter" won't remove the bad memories far enough from her mind.

Fall nights in New England can get very cold, and it was especially cold the night Maggie was called out to see a man about a burglar. Believing there was a burglar in his house he put his scantily dressed kids in the car and drove off to meet the officers. Arriving on scene, the officers wrapped the children in blankets, called child protective services, and proceeded to the house to check things out.

They arrived at the trailer to find it filthy, with dirty diapers in huge piles; the only sign of joy was the half-lit string of Christmas lights on the porch. There was no burglar, and it appeared there was no hope for the children.

Maggie has been on the job thirty years now, but when she was a rookie child endangerment laws weren't what they are today. There wasn't as much guidance or structure to follow when happening upon a scene such as this one. When her sergeant and child protection arrived on scene, they decided it was best to have the father take them to their grandmother's house for the evening and they would sort things out the next day.

It was late, Maggie's shift was ending, and she wanted to get home. Child services had arrived in a pick-up truck and there was no room for the children. Maggie could have stayed to drive the children in her cruiser, but she was new. She assumed that social services or the supervisors on scene would transport the children. Maggie left. The father put the children back into his car and headed toward the grandmother's house; child services and the sergeant following behind them.

Less than ten minutes later Maggie heard the screams of the sergeant over the radio calling for assistance; the father had driven his car directly into an oncoming truck, killing the children. Maggie can't remember if the father was killed. She only remembers the children.

At this scene, there were no screaming parents mourning the loss of their children; there was shocked silence. There are too many scenes with mourners, and those are also hard to fit through the holes in the sieve, especially when you are the officer responsible for them.

Thirty years later, Maggie never leaves early. She never rushes back to the station at the end of a shift. She is hyper-vigilant when children are involved. She blames herself and believes she was selfish to leave the scene, that she could have stopped the father from putting the children in the car and changed the outcome.

One night Maggie was called to a scene where a baby was walking down the highway in diapers and was almost hit by three different vehicles. They found the home of the child, and what they discovered was another sad situation. The baby's grandfather was also its father; the mother had three children and was pregnant again and the grandmother was mentally ill. Maggie called social services while the rookie she was training was instructed not to let any of the adults go back into the house. In her experience, when social services arrive on scene, if there's a gun in the house it will be pointed at the officers.

She was right. The grandfather produced a gun, and the pregnant mother and one of the children charged the police. Maggie was able to diffuse the situation safely, only to hear social services was going to leave the kids with their mother. Maggie disagreed, and they were able to reach a judge and have the children placed in protective custody based on the filthy condition of the house and the behavior of the adults in the home. "All I could think of was that asshole that killed his children. Not again. I'm not letting this happen again. Not again."

Officers aren't just responding to calls; they are taking care of people on scene, they are trying to keep everything together and make the pieces fall into place so hysteria doesn't break out. It's not easy.

The summers are as hot as the winters are cold in New England, and people flock to pools and beaches to cool off, never expecting tragedy to strike. When a four-year-old drowned in a crowded pool and no one noticed until it was too late, Maggie simply had to transport the mother and the babysitter to the hospital. Just drive. All the while the mother was pleading with Maggie to save her child, begging her to say her son was going to be alright. Maggie knew once the mother left the car, her life would change forever and there wasn't anything she could do about it.

Sometimes, by a cruel twist of fate, a parent comes upon the accident scene of their beloved child. They're on their way home; you are blocking the road, telling them they have to seek an alternate route because of a motorcycle accident. They're an attractive couple in their late 40's, their son has a motorcycle and he was headed this way. *Can you please find out if it's our son? Please?*

You can't let them through to the scene. You try stalling. You don't want it to be their son. *Please?* You confirm the identity of the deceased and tell his parents, "Yes, I am so sorry, it is your son." The father falls to his knees and lets out an inhuman wail while the mother stares at you in shock, tears dripping down her face. You are Maggie, witnessing a man lose himself in utter and complete grief.

She can't seem to escape the grief. A father and his 13-year-old son were playing ball with his two daughters nearby; the mother wasn't home as they are getting divorced. When the father ran inside to get a few things done, his son hung himself from a tree in their yard. Maggie and the paramedics arrived on scene, and while the paramedics were working on the teen, Maggie was left to speak to the father. She knew the boy wasn't going to make it, but the father was pleading with her to tell him that his son will be okay. She didn't know what to say, so she simply looked the man in the face and told him they were doing the best they could.

Whatever precipitated the divorce was now irrelevant; any bills that needed to be paid or housework that needed to be done no longer mattered. "I don't know how people go on with their lives after these incidents. I really don't. The parents are looking at you and pleading with you as if you have a special power and you can give them back their child. When they are doing that they take part of your soul forever. And it's a terrible feeling and that is the only way I can explain it to you. The wailing, the crying is inhuman and you have a job to do through all of that. Then you go home and how do you deal with that? How was my day?"

Maggie cries as she tells these stories, and she has to pause often to compose herself. She does it daily and has become good at it. Watching grown men deflate and cry when they hear bad news is very profound, and it's something first responders witness all too often. It's a feeling of defeat, the same feeling the doctors and nurses have when the child is delivered to them and there is nothing they can do. Maggie gets to walk away from the trauma, but the trauma never walks away from her.

When Maggie witnesses adults dying, it's different. It's traumatic, but it's not the same as when a child dies. It makes no sense at all, least of all to the parents. "Parents take part of your physical energy, part of you leaves you, and they take it from you. It's terrible. It's terrible. And we go home. We feed the dogs. How do you talk about your day? It's easier not to. You have to separate the two. It doesn't get easier. Ever."

Not everyone dies, though; sometimes police are able to find solutions that save everyone. Those moments are the ones they want to hold on to. Those are the memories they don't filter out. One weekday morning, Maggie was dispatched to a call where someone in the house was threatening his mother with a knife. Other than knowing he wouldn't put the knife down, she didn't have much information. She still remembers the cul-de-sac, the deep driveway, and the blue door of the house standing slightly ajar.

As the sergeant on scene, Maggie approached the door and announced their presence; they received no response. After multiple fruitless attempts to make contact, Maggie announced they'd be entering the house. They found a 20-year-old male named Dave holding a Bible in one hand and a large butcher knife in the other; he didn't speak or acknowledge their presence. His mother was distraught, she said her son hadn't slept in two days, wouldn't speak to her, and she didn't know what was wrong with him.

With guns drawn, Maggie tried to reach Dave. Shifting his weight back and forth, he continued to ignore her. Maggie is now in someone's home with a distraught parent, a non-responsive son with a weapon, and officers looking to her for guidance.

"I keep thinking, I may have to take this kid's life. I may have to shoot this kid. If he lunges toward us with the knife, I am going to have to shoot. I could feel the pulse pounding in my neck and knew I had to make some quick decisions. I slowed my breathing and my actions; I talked to myself while talking to the kid. I read a book about combat breathing and how important it is in these situations to control your breathing so you can control yourself.

"It was almost like watching myself from above. I'm in this terrible situation but I need to think clearly. I need to remove myself from it while staying in it so I can think clearly. I remember thinking, *This is it. If he steps or makes any movement toward me I will have to pull the trigger.* I had to tell myself I am justified but I don't want to kill this kid. I made peace with that in my mind while I am outwardly saying, 'Please put the knife down. It's not worth it. Why are you doing this? Please, if you move forward we will need to take action, please don't make us do that.'

"This is what I've trained for over and over; this is what I'm sworn to do, and this is the situation I am in. There are cops that never have this experience. I've read about it, I've heard about it from other cops and here I am. I had to make myself okay with taking a life if I needed to."

While Maggie was struggling with what to do, she heard more officers and an ambulance arrive. She had no Taser; they weren't allowed to have them because a suspect died after being tazed while high on cocaine. The irony of the situation wasn't lost on her: she wanted to find a non-lethal solution but the most convenient method wasn't available to her. The only thing she had was a bean bag rifle, which was in her cruiser.

The decision whether or not to retrieve the rifle wasn't an easy one. Did she take a chance and go get it? As a supervisor she needed to make a decision and now she felt there were enough officers on the scene to cover her and that she could end it without killing him. She knew it was a risk, but the situation had been going on for fifteen minutes with no progress; it was the only chance for everyone to make it out alive.

Asking someone to bring the rifle in wasn't an option; Dave would hear her and possibly react. She couldn't risk it. Slowly, she made her way outside while two other officers continued talking to Dave.

Squinting from the bright sun, Maggie could see the ambulance staging and more cars arriving. She knew everything rested on whether or not she could disarm the man without incident.

Maggie walked behind a tall officer so Dave wouldn't see her rifle and made her way to a position where she could see him but he couldn't see her. One person she couldn't hide the rifle from was his mother. The mother immediately escalated the situation, saying, "You're not going to shoot my baby;

you aren't going to shoot my son," while positioning herself between Dave and the officers.

Things went from bad to worse and Dave looked around in a state of heightened agitation; he saw Maggie. He now realized the gravity of the situation and said, "Okay, I'll make a deal with you, everyone just get back." Everyone took a step back except Dave and Maggie, and, with a clear shot, Maggie fired and hit him in the ribs. His shirt and skin ripped causing him to bleed, and Maggie quickly advanced and told him to get on the ground. He tried to run instead; Maggie then shot him in the thigh sending him to the ground.

As the officers arrested Dave and loaded him into the ambulance to get checked out, his mother began to scream at the officers asking what they were doing with her son. "Why are you arresting him? He didn't do anything!"

"I kept thinking, 'Are you kidding me? What do you think is going to happen if you call the police to your house and there is a weapon in someone's hand?'"

With everything wrapped up at the scene, Maggie got back in her cruiser and finished her shift. There was no debriefing, no break, no time off. Simply back to work; no time to decompress. What she needed was to go home and take a break, not get right back onto the street; she was physically and emotionally drained.

She was also a folk hero; the good guys won. There was no media frenzy in the press, no one died. They had no use for the situation. The only people that cared were her fellow officers, and even then it was in the uncomfortable manner law enforcement holds on to their heroes; they're hoping that someday they will also be the ones that walk away from a situation.

Everyone wanted to hear what happened, what she was thinking, and how she decided to take the chance and get the rifle. She tried not to embellish as she told and retold the story. The more she told the story the worse she felt about it. She needed a debriefing, maybe; she needed something, but she didn't know exactly what. Would she seem like a baby if she asked for help? Was it just her? Was she over-reacting? No one offered her a hand so she thought what she was experiencing was routine and she should handle it herself. After all, she used force on a suspect, proved she could handle herself as a supervisor and a female officer. She could handle this.

Couldn't she?

Maggie's been through a lot of counseling over the years, and sometimes it was more like having coffee and writing a large check. Not everyone can provide the counsel officers need; it takes time to find the right person. Maggie also found it helpful to attend counseling with her husband, as it gave her a platform to speak and be heard by him.

Maggie needed her husband Ben to understand how hard it was to shut off her work persona when she got home. She needed him to understand her way of thinking.

At work, things are black and white when it comes to getting things done. You simply do it, because if you don't someone could get killed, hurt, or sued. The stakes are much higher when answering a call than if she forgets to pick up milk on the way home. That's how it is for Maggie, although that's not how Ben sees or feels things. "I saw someone with their head blown off today and you're upset because I forgot milk?" Maggie can't always give the desired reaction to every day issues because she has to shut off so much emotion on the job. If a police officer felt everything they experience, it would be impossible to live.

Maggie does have one outlet. She finds solace in her time with the Honor Guard. She loves being part of something that honors the people that gave everything to their communities. "It's very important to me to know that feeling of someone who gave their all. It's not a sacrifice for me to put that uniform on, it's an honor. But I put it on knowing I may be preparing for death."

It's always been important to her, though she doesn't know why; it just is. As the years go on, it's more important than ever before, not only to honor and keep watch over the officer you're burying, but simply to do the right thing. "It's the only way that I personally know how to say thank you, that can I give back that's of no monetary or tangible value."

So what would Maggie say to a rookie if she had all the time in the world to talk to them?

"Your job is to make sure that people are safe, the law is upheld, and things get done properly. Don't take things at face value and make dumb mistakes. There are options. You don't have to take everyone to jail. Be smart about it.

"Emotions on the job may be black and white so you can survive, but there is a lot of gray area. The choices that are made could cost someone their life. It's an important voice to have in your head — the one that's telling you that there is more than one possible outcome.

"You need to stay focused, calm and methodical; that will come with time. Take advantage of every training opportunity, and fall back on it; you'll need to be prepared.

"We don't have super powers. Even Superman couldn't do some of the stuff we do and we're human. It's pretty amazing that you signed up for this.

"I can't tell you what you are going to see, but I will tell you this: if you don't need to see a dead body, don't look at it. You will see it for the rest of your life.

"Finally, you are not a cop. You are John Doe. Your *job* is to be a cop. It's not your identity. Try to learn the difference; you'll never make it otherwise."

JOHN

John has protected himself much better than Maggie has, or so he thinks. He likes to think he is more of an open drain than a sieve, letting everything go in an effort to protect himself, retaining nothing. He's actually done the opposite: he hasn't let anything go. He's buried it deep within himself, and, until recently, has been unable to open up to anyone.

As with most officers, early on John felt something inside him that liked the idea of becoming a police officer and wanted to help the people of San Francisco; having an officer speak to his high school class sealed things for him. He went to college with an eye on becoming a police officer someday. John found himself working corrections for five years first; however, spending his time locked up with criminals, breaking up fights and opening and closing cell doors wasn't as appealing as being on the street making a difference before the crime happened.

When John was accepted onto the San Francisco Police Department, it was a dream come true. Starry-eyed with a vision of helping everyone he came into contact with and being loved by them, he began what would become a career filled with the stuff of horror movies. He quickly found it was the rare occasion when he could protect someone before a crime, and not everyone would love him and he certainly couldn't help everyone.

John's biggest problem was his route: he worked in what was called the Tenderloin for eighteen years, and he had the unenviable position of seeing people die in every way imaginable. Some more memorable than others, not only for the way they died, but for the circumstances surrounding their deaths.

Called to the scene of a person on a ledge, John was disgusted with what he found before he even trudged up the ten floors to try to help. A Grateful Dead concert had just gotten out and the crowd had gathered at the base of a building. A naked girl danced along the edge. The crowd called for her to jump. Angry, John wanted to silence the crowd who seemed to think a body splintering on the sidewalk would be enjoyable, but he had a life to save so he moved past them into the building.

On the roof, one officer spoke to the girl while John tried to approach her. He couldn't grab onto anything to pull her back because she was naked; she was also high on crystal meth. As the crowd continued to call for her to jump, the girl glanced toward her boyfriend who was sitting on the ground nearby, waved to the officers, and said, "Bye, bye." She swan dived off the building.

John had always seen the bodies after they had hit the pavement; this was the first time he actually witnessed someone jumping. He didn't want to watch her make her quick descent toward death, but for some reason, he couldn't help himself. As he listened to the boyfriend crying, he watched her body hit the pavement and heard the collective gasp of the crowd and then the silence. The crowd had gotten what they wanted and they likely wouldn't forget it.

Containing his anger and frustration, John headed toward the exit and stopped to comfort the boyfriend, but words seemed meaningless at a time like this. For John, emotions wouldn't help either, so he held them in check, passed the body, which was covered by a yellow tarp, and headed back to his shift. It wasn't his district, his report, or his responsibility anymore.

It still lives in his memory, and, though one may try, one can't bury them forever. After a shooting he was involved in, he and the other officers were given three days off and expected to come back ready to work with no obvious signs of trauma; easier said than done. Flashbacks happen. After his shooting, the first call John received was for a man with a gun. He immediately thought of the incident that had sent him home for a few days' rest.

Details are easy to remember: the rain pouring down, a few guys out sick that day, and the look on the face of the bank president when he saw the officers enter. John knew it was preferable for officers to stay outside a bank if there was an alarm; the last thing they wanted was a shootout. This time there was no alarm, just the report of a suspicious looking person, so they went in.

The suspect held a grenade in each hand. As the officers entered, the president's eyes widened, a look of mingled panic and relief spread over his face. Seeing the police, the suspect grabbed the president around the neck and held a grenade to his ear.

"Back out, I'm going to kill him!"

"We aren't going anywhere; put the grenade down and let's talk."

Suddenly coming alive, the bank customers ran for cover screaming. The suspect began to back away from the officers, and, as he did, he tripped and fell. The president raced away.

By now, eight officers had entered the bank. Perhaps sensing his time was running out, the suspect pulled the pin from a grenade and raised his arm to throw it, prompting the officers to fire at him. Ignoring the gaping hole in his neck created by the bullets, he threw the grenades and tried to begin assembling what looked like Molotov cocktails.

When the suspect finally fell, never to get up, the officers found he had taken the powder out of World War II grenades. They were impotent. The Molotov cocktails were bottles filled with water. They would never know why the man had subjected a bank full of innocent people to such a dramatic scene, but his death would be ruled "Suicide by Cop," and the officers who fired their weapons would go home knowing their bullets killed another human being. It defied logic.

Looking back, John can pinpoint when he realized that perhaps he wasn't handling things as well as he should. Four days before Thanksgiving in 1993, John was training a rookie when they were sent to a reported suicide call. After receiving no answer to their knock on the door, they turned the handle to find it unlocked. Knowing what he would find, John sent the rookie in first. Simply put, John was tired of looking at dead bodies.

He may have been tired, but he still had a job to do. An elderly man had shot himself in the head; there was a gun to secure and a scene to process. While waiting for the coroner to arrive, John found that the victim had laid his personal papers on the kitchen table in an effort to make things easier for the first responders. He also left them a note apologizing for putting them through this, for subjecting them to a bloody corpse with half a skull and the remnants of his previously engaged mind all over the wall.

After writing the reports and eating dinner, John and his trainee went back onto the road handling calls for the rest of their shift. Business as usual; just another dead body.

Sent to an apartment because of a bad smell, John believed this call would be his fifth dead body in three days. The body appeared stiff from rigor mortis and the air was filled with the smell of decay and human waste; John didn't even check for a pulse. He had become so immune to death. Death wasn't present at this scene, though; a sudden moaning sound startled John and his partner. The victim had had a stroke and had been in that position for three days.

By now, John had fifteen years on the job, and many dead bodies had crossed his path – stabbings, shootings, accidents and more. He had lost something along the way. In an effort to regain it, he was sent back to the academy for training.

Shortly after returning, he was called to yet another scene of a person with a gun. This time the officers were dispatched to the wrong apartment number. Four officers stood in a room trying to find out the correct location when the door opened behind John. A mentally ill woman now had a gun to his head. He quickly diffused the situation and eventually received a commendation for his ability to resolve it without violence. He went back to work the next night, as usual, as though nothing extraordinary had happened.

Thus began the period of time when John forgot how to speak normally to people, his temper flared, and he began to put on weight. He doesn't recall feeling depressed, didn't know what PTSI was, had no motivation but studied for promotions, took the tests and didn't care if he passed or failed.

Until he realized what he had become.

One dead baby changed everything.

That night John was paired with a young man who had just spent a year in seminary; a good guy who decided he also wanted to help people by becoming a law enforcement officer. Dispatched to a call for a baby who wasn't breathing, they arrived to chaos.

It was a newer apartment house, clean and neat, except for the baby on the floor, the father rocking in his chair, his wife on her knees before him sobbing and saying, "I'm sorry," and the four other children scattered throughout the room crying.

John and another officer began mouth to mouth and chest compressions, but their efforts were futile; the baby had been dead at least an hour. They now had to restore order and make sense of the situation. Before they could, the mother ran to the window and attempted to throw herself out; John's partner was quick enough to grab her before she did.

Both parents were admitted for psychological exams; they had become incoherent and unresponsive. The children were checked out and placed in the hands of social services. John and his partner went back to their car to find the burritos they picked up for dinner earlier were now soggy and inedible.

John was pissed his dinner was ruined and began to wonder what that said about him as a person. Was he directing his anger toward his burrito instead of the family of the baby? He knew it was time to take a step back and think about what was important, but he was afraid to. He didn't know if showing compassion would make him go crazy. Until now, he had been focusing on self-preservation.

"It's just the way it is, it's my life, it was my job. I didn't do anything extraordinary. You have to survive and go do your job. If you are worried about things you see on the street it's going to go bad for you," John said. "I never thought about it. I went to work, did what I had to do, and went home."

Home meant his wife and kids. The wife he met on one of his better days two years into his job. Walking the foot-beat during Fleet Week, his partner received a call from his girlfriend telling him she was going to escort her friend to the docks so she could meet some sailors. John's partner didn't want his girlfriend anywhere near the sailors and told her to stay home. He abruptly hung up, looked at John and said, 'That's how you get your point across to your girl."

Not exactly. A short time later he saw his girlfriend walking around the docks and they got into a heated argument. John hid out in a doorway waiting for them to finish. The door opened, a girl walked out and they struck up a conversation. She found

John's predicament amusing and they quickly established a relationship that would eventually lead to marriage.

John was always honest with his wife; he worked nights, holidays, and overtime leaving her to raise the kids most of the time. He told her when they first met that this was his life; he had baggage. He would understand if she couldn't handle it. Law enforcement was what he did; he knew it would take a toll on her.

He didn't take it home with him or get mad at anybody because he knew it wouldn't do anyone any good and his kids wouldn't have understood. He never went to work worrying about getting shot or dying, and it never felt futile; he always hoped he was going to help someone.

After thirty years on the job, John retired. He spent that last ten years in the traffic division; twenty years on the street was enough. He couldn't physically keep up with the other guys anymore; the job had passed him by.

Nowadays, he reads a lot, watches the History Channel, walks his dog, and enjoys his family. He also offers simple advice to all the rookies out there.

"Go to work and give it the best you can but leave it there. Don't bring it home. No need to go out drinking or take things personal. Go home and go to bed, play with your kids, do what you have to do. Don't dwell on things. You're gonna see a lot of this. Get used to it or quit. I always realized it was my job. I'm sure I'm scarred; it will scar you too. Find a way to cope; there are more resources for you than there ever were for me."

Part Eight

AJAX

When asking officers to tell me their stories, I received an e-mail from an officer telling me he had nothing I could use. I thought about it for months and it wasn't until Jeff introduced the Sophocles Concept you read about in the first chapter that I realized how we could use him. What he wrote in an e-mail to me is below; he is Ajax. We realized that what he said ties beautifully into the Sophocles Concept and, to keep the integrity of what he said, we have kept his e-mail as he has written it. These are the words of an officer you may pass on the street today.

What is wrong with a person that puts on a gun and vest every day and goes and sees what we see and then keeps getting up and doing it every day? What is wrong with someone that they would continue doing it? The average person would say, "I am not doing that again!" What's wrong with us?

I know that I am not alone in dealing with the dark side of our lives. The problem is finding a healthy coping mechanism. I readily admit that medication is not the answer and I believe that in some ways it restricts healing.

My marriage is amazing. I have a wife who is holding a candle on the edge of my darkness coaxing me continually into the revitalizing glow.

The Lord has blessed us in so many ways. The issues that I deal with are related to my career. Notice that I did not use the term job. To me it is a disservice to all of us who sacrifice so much. Sacrifice, the one word that I would use to describe what ails so many of us in this career. It is the center of that thin blue line which links all of us. Whether the sacrifice is being away from family so much or an injury with lasting and sometimes debilitating effects for the rest of our lives. Of course the ultimate sacrifice is a line of duty death.

The career is rife with small sacrifices that occur daily. Throughout our time of service, long after the shiny badge begins to dull, those small sacrifices chip away at the armor that is required to survive the profession. As that protective layer erodes, it is unable to withstand the constant barrage and causes fissures allowing injury to our souls. In the end, what you will see is the punch line to so many jokes about the profession. The drastically different extremes between the wet eared rookie who sees the good in people and the short tempered crusty veteran who views everyone with skepticism and suspicion.

That description leads to where I am currently. One third of the way through my career, my ears should still be a little moist; however, every day I dress in my blues, I feel myself identifying with the surly veteran. Everyone has an angle. The department is out to get me. My family doesn't understand.

The public is waiting to crucify me at the slightest misstep. Help I'm drowning in a sea of frustration.

This, this is what leads to professional burn out. I have personally borne the caskets of a friend and two comrades to their final resting places. I can't do that again. On three separate occasions I have had to fight for my life, deciding in milliseconds whether to take their lives or sacrifice mine. How many more times can I confront the devil's henchmen before my hands won't be fast enough or my aim is not true? My body is permanently scarred and deformed from injuries in the line of duty. So that others may live. These have been the swift blows to my armor allowing the corrosion of sacrifice to latch on and eat it away. My flesh has been exposed. All of that in a short nine years. In a town of 27,000 people.

I still have two thirds of my career left. I am crouching, twisting, and sucking in my gut to hide behind the remainder of the fragile pieces protecting me. How do I heal my armor? I know it will never be as whole and spit-shined as it once was. If it's not restored, will I make it to retirement with my sanity? Or will I stumble and fall onto my sword, in sacrifice?

I appreciate any moment you spend reading this more than you could ever know. For some reason putting my thoughts on this subject into words feels as though I have welded shut one more fissure.

I looked at some of the stories you have included in your book so far and pondered where mine could be included. I'm not so sure that it can be. I'm not confined to a wheel chair and I haven't been shot in the face. You asked for one event that would open a window to the public about sacrifices in law enforcement. I really don't have one that fits with all of these other examples you have provided. My sacrifices are not nearly to their level.

I am in a dark place with my attitude towards law enforcement. As I said, my attitude has been shaped over my nine years of service. From a multitude of events. Of those, I believe I have had more emotional and social trouble than physical damage to my body.

Please remember, I carried the caskets of three fellow officers who died horrible deaths in the line of duty. Two of them were personally known to me. I stood emotionless at the head and foot of those caskets while family and friends wept and sobbed. All the while, I have a litany of thoughts and emotions charging through me. I had to quit the Honor Guard after that because I knew I could not do that again. It was impossible for me to keep from exploring my own mortality involving this chosen career while listening to those loved ones begging for the return of those lost souls.

Then one day while visiting family, I learn that a very close friend, the photographer of my wedding and a US Marshall Task Force member has been shot multiple times while on duty. I sat at the hospital with his family waiting for an opportunity to see him. When I finally do get to see him, we can't do much more than shake hands because he has to write everything down because of the breathing tube shoved down his throat.

I will tell you this. That event was extremely hard for me emotionally because I worked at the same department as both of his brothers. My first day on the job was Christmas Day. That day I was away from my family. However, my new family, my family in blue, invited me to their house for Christmas dinner. The whole family was very nice and welcoming and that is a gesture that I will always be thankful for. Therefore, years later, I was there in the waiting room of the hospital with that same family trying to console and do anything I could to help them.

I believe that those events coupled with all of the other day to day emotional shots of the job contributed to my view of this career. Those events are the only ones that I believe are different from what the masses have dealt with in their career.

Not only have I dealt with the emotional side, but the physical side.

Five weeks prior to my wedding, I was pursuing a vehicle traveling upwards of 90mph in downtown. A fellow officer turned around on the suspect vehicle in front of me and lost control of his vehicle on the wet roadway. To avoid a T-bone collision, I attempted to steer around him causing my vehicle to hydroplane. My vehicle eventually came to rest after I had struck an oak tree head on at approximately 70mph.

My vehicle at the time was equipped with a brush guard which caused a delay in the airbag deployment. I vividly remember my face striking the steering wheel as the airbag exploded. I also took a side impact to the right side of my forehead by the laptop computer. To this day, I still have neck and back issues. The workers comp doctor said they could not do anything else to help me and that my body had recovered to the best that it could. I recently had sinus surgery due to a deviated septum and a bone spur, all a result of this crash; however, workers comp would not have paid for it.

Four weeks prior to being the best man in a fellow officer's wedding, I responded to a family disturbance. I had been dispatched 30 minutes prior to being off duty and as the backup officer. I arrived on scene first and approached the residence. I was met in the driveway by the suspect who I later learned was the son of the complainant. I was able to see his father standing behind a closed glass storm door. The suspect seemed to be acting erratically and kept trying to shake my hand. I continually told him to step away from me as I tried to maintain some kind of distance between us. Eventually, after not listening, I grasped his extended arm and attempted to detain him. A physical altercation resulted.

During the altercation, I tried multiple times to either force him to the ground or lock up his arm. He was able to strike me several times in the face. I disengaged and attempted to shove him away from me in order to reengage in a different manner. As I shoved him away, he flipped around and grabbed my arm. He then horse kicked my right leg breaking it. I tried to step into his body to shove him off and heard further breaking of my bone. Due to the pain, I began falling to my knees and I drew my weapon. While splayed on the ground, holding myself up with my left arm and left knee, I pointed my weapon at the suspect who was just a couple of feet in front of me and used the ten code no officer likes to use or hear over the radio. I told him to lie down on the ground. He stood over me with his fists in front of him ready to continue on. I explained that if he even motioned towards me I would kill him. After several moments of staring at each other, he eventually complied and lay on the ground.

To my left I kept hearing his father calling to me attempting to come out of the house. I told him to stay where he was or I would shoot him too. The suspect was continually taunting me calling me names. After what seemed like an eternity, a backup officer arrived on scene and took the suspect into custody. The original case officer eventually arrived, fourth on scene.

I am reminded every day when I get out of bed about that incident. The ligaments in my ankle stretched causing a tendency to be unstable while moving quickly. I already have arthritis in it which will only get worse over time.

I explained previously that I view each law enforcement professional as being covered in a coat of armor. My view is that each of these emotional events causes dents, cracks, and then chips away at that bright shining armor from your first day on the job. To the point that all of the events you survive throughout your career eventually begin damaging your soul. Some of us professionals survive twenty-five to thirty years of this. Others, the damage is so extensive so early in their career that their soul can't stand up to the constant barrage and they escape the career. I know enough career professionals who have retired from the job. I can say without a doubt, that those who spent the majority of their career on the front lines and not hiding under their desk behind a closed door are just as emotionally damaged as those who chose to escape.

Part Nine

EPILOGUE

Those of us who maintain a dangerous life-style will experience fear and anxiety. But, to do so, allows us to join a fraternity of those who have, since the beginning of man's time, endured...They endured. We endured. Is it the cost of the privilege of such company.

- Paul Whitesell

The law enforcement world is almost entirely made up of Type A personalities which are known for having to be in control of every situation all the time and think requesting help is a sign of weakness. Law enforcement officers have it ingrained into them from the earliest days of the basic recruit academy they are to be in control of each crime scene they respond to and this will allow them to meet any challenge and stay alive (Blum, 2001). One of the biggest hurdles to change will be teaching the law enforcement community to accept psychological injuries from traumatic events are a real threat to officers and that early intervention is the key to recovery. Early intervention requires either a request for help or clear agency policy requiring intervention following a traumatic incident. The stigma attached to officers who seek psychological treatment is still alive and well despite the progress made with public awareness of the problems associated with posttraumatic stress disorder. Fear of damaging a reputation is not an issue for officers who seek treatment for physical trauma, which is an accepted part of combat. Making a change in the belief system that psychological injuries are also an accepted part of combat will be a challenge. Like the progress made in the medical field in the treatment of physical trauma, enormous strides have been made in the treatment of psychological trauma. However, law enforcement officers must make timely use of these services to obtain the greatest benefit.

Officers who have been traumatized believe in post-traumatic stress and all the associated side effects while some others may be skeptical of its existence or treatment (Artwohl & Christensen, 1997). The initial evidence has been developed from military units supporting the use of peer supporters and debriefings, and more accurate long-term research into the use of these techniques with law enforcement officers could further push agency administrators into adopting these techniques to assist their officers. Future research should also focus on trying to identify other preventative measures and risk factors which could be either developed in the officers or sought out during the initial portion of the officer selection process to create a more resilient workforce. Additional research should also focus on developing clear guidelines for the treatment of psychological injuries.

While changes are being made in the thinking of new front line patrol officers who have grown up accustomed to hearing about PTSD in the news and the progress that has been made in its treatment, it will still be some time before these officers are in each agency must buy into the concept of traumatic stress injuries now, recognize the danger they pose to officers, and respond quickly and appropriately. Changing the mindset of an entire institution will be daunting but in the long run will result in a better officer, a better agency, and a community more satisfied with the service both renders.

While the studies here have focused on law enforcement officers specifically, the same chronic and critical incident stress is seen in firefighters, emergency medical technicians, paramedics, and dispatchers for each of the above groups. Sophocles identified the signs and symptoms of traumatic stress injuries well before the world understood the science surrounding how the mind works. Ajax returned home a different man than when he had left. The trauma of war had caused changes in Ajax and these changes cost him his life. While Sophocles wasn't clear as to the cause of Ajax's actions, the effects described are very evident and can be related to today's soldiers, law enforcement officers, and other first responders who bring calm in a chaotic world at the cost of their own physical and psychological well-being. Each of these first responders face the troubles of society; all the while controlling their emotions so they can complete the assigned task. The problem is emotions are never completely controlled; they are just buried for a short time and will come back to the surface. Any law enforcement agency's failure to adopt policy to address traumatic stress injuries is the equivalent of not adopting a policy on the treatment of physical trauma. Both are life threatening and both are issues that will change not only the officer directly affected, but also cause collateral damage that is far reaching.

The loss of an officer due to physical or mental injury is devastating to a community, an agency, and a family. Officers plan and train more often to address the physical injury as a result of their work, but it is the psychological strains that are more likely to damage the family, end the career, or the life of an officer. We must stand with those who stand for us. We have the knowledge to improve officer effectiveness, mental health, and survivability. We have the obligation to help the collateral damage that is left in the wake of an officer injury. It is all of our responsibility and we must act now. Our protectors thank you.

Notes

Artwohl, A. (2002, October). Perceptual and
    Memory Distortion During Officer Involved
    Shootings. *FBI Law Enforcement Bulletin,*
    71(10), 18.

Artwohl, A., & Christensen, L. W. (1997). *Deadly*
    Force Encounters: What Cops Need To Know To
    Mentally And Physically Prepare For And
    Survive A Gunfight . Boulder, CO: Paladin
    Press.

Blum, L. (2001). *Force Under Pressure: How Cops Live*
    and Why They Die. New York, NY: Lantern
    Books.

Carlier, I. V., Lamberts, R. D., & Gersons, B. P.
    (1997, August). Risk Factors for
    Posttraumatic Stress Symptomatology in
    Police Officers: a Prospective Analysis. *The*
    Journal of Nervous and Mental Disease, 185(8),
    498-506. doi:10.1097/00005053-199708000-
    00004

Clark, D. W. (2012, May). Law Enforcement
    Suicide: Current Knowledge and Future
    Directions. *The Police Chief,* 48-51.

Dowling F.G., M. G. (2006). A Peer-Based
    Assistance Program for Officers with the
    New York City Police Department: Report of

the Effects of Sept. 11, 2001. *American Journal of Psychiatry, 163*(1), 151-153.

Faust, K. L., & Ven, T. V. (2014, June). Policing Disaster: An Analytical Review of the Literature on Policing, Disaster, and Post-traumatic Stress Disorder. *Sociology Compass, 8*(6), 614-626. doi:10.1111/soc4.12160

Federal Bureau of Investigation. (2012, September). *Crime in the United States 2012*. Retrieved from FBI.gov: http://www.fbi.gov/about-us/cjis/ucr/crime-in-the-u.s/2012/crime-in-the-u.s.-2012/tables/1tabledatadecoverviewpdf/tabl e_1_crime_in_the_united_states_by_volume _and_rate_per_100000_inhabitants_1993-2012.xls

Grossman, D., & Christensen, L. W. (2008). *On Combat, The Psychology and Physiology of Deadly Conflict in War and in Peace*. Belleville, IL: Warrior Science Publications.

Kamienski, L. (2013). Helping the Postmodern Ajax is Managing Combat Trauma through Pharmacology a Faustian Bargain? *Armed Forces and Society*, 395-414.

Kates, A. R. (1999). *CopShock: Surviving PostTraumatic Stress Disorder*. Tucson, AZ: Holbrook Street Press.

Minnesota, S. o. (2015). *2015 Minnesota Statutes*. Retrieved from 353.656 Disability Benefits

Subdivision
4(b)(2):https://www.revisor.mn.gov/statute
s?id=353.656&year=2015 Subdivision

Mitchell, J. T., & Everly Jr., G. S. (1996). *Critical Incident Stress Debriefing: An Operations Manual for Cisd, Defusing and Other Group Crisis Intervention Services*. Columbia, MA: Chevron Publishing Corporation.

Paton, D. (2009). *Traumatic Stress in Police Officers: A Career-length Assessment from Recruitment to Retirement*. Springfield, IL: Charles C. Thomas Publisher Ltd.

Prati, G., & Pietrantoni, L. (2010, April). Risk and Resilience Factors Among Italian Municipal Police Officers Exposed to Critical Incidents. *Journal of Police and Criminal Psychology*, 25(1), 27-33.

Stratton, J., Parker, D., & Snibbe, J. (1984). Post-Traumatic Stress: Study of Police Officers Involved in Shootings. *Psychological Reports*, 55(1), 127-31. doi:10.2466/pr0.1984.55.1.127

Taylor, M., Markham, A., Reis, J., Padilla, G., Potterat, E., Drummond, S., & Mujica-Parodi, L. (2008, August). Physical Fitness Influences Stress Reactions to Extreme Military Training. *Military Medicine, 173*(8), 738-42.

Resources

www.BlueHELP.org

ABOUT THE AUTHORS

Jeffrey M. McGill

Jeff began his law enforcement career in the military, serving as a Security Police Officer. Following four years of military service, he entered civilian law enforcement at the Okaloosa County Sheriff's Office where he stayed full time for 15 years. Jeff had numerous assignments including, patrol, street crimes, beach/marine unit, investigations, sex offender unit, and gang intelligence. During his time with the Sheriff's Office Jeff also spent six years assigned as a Task Force Officer for the US Marshal's Violent Fugitive Task Force based in Pensacola, FL. Jeff is now a full time Training Coordinator/Instructor for the police academy located on the Northwest Florida State College.

He is the co-founder of Type A Solutions a training company focused on the needs of first responders. He volunteers as a peer supporter for critical incident debriefings.

Jeff has received numerous awards for actions taken during an officer involved shooting where his partner was severely injured in the line of duty. The story was told in *Hearts Beneath the Badge*.

Jeff earned a Bachelor's Degree in Criminal Justice with a minor in Psychology from Troy University and a Master's Degree in Criminal Justice from Arizona State University. He is currently a PhD student at Nova Southeastern University.

Karen Solomon

Since 2014, Karen has been giving a voice to the thousands of officers in the field who can't or won't speak out. Karen is the co-Founder of <u>Blue H.E.L.P.</u> and the creator of <u>1stHelp.net</u>. She has interviewed hundreds of law enforcement officers and their families to gain insight into the field, trauma, stress, and both physical and emotional survival. Karen is a national speaker, author, columnist and advocate. Married to a police officer for sixteen years, Karen understands today's challenges and puts her knowledge to work on behalf of the entire profession. Karen has a bachelor's degree in Political Science from Eckerd College.